Carleton
Memories

Carleton Memories

Catherine Rothwell
Sept. 2008

Catherine Rothwell

First published in the United Kingdom in 2008 by

Bank House Books

BIC House

1 Christopher Road

East Grinstead

West Sussex

RH19 3BT

www.bankhousebooks.com

© Catherine Rothwell, 2008

British Library Cataloguing in Publication Data
A catalogue record for this book is available from the British Library.

ISBN 9781904408390

Typesetting and origination by Bank House Books
Printed and bound by Lightning Source.

CONTENTS

Introduction   1

Chapter One: Early Days   3

Chapter Two: Fylde Families   21

Chapter Three: Daily Life   27

Chapter Four: Carleton Parish   31

Chapter Five: Farms and Farmers   36

Chapter Six: Windmills   41

Chapter Seven: Schools   53

Chapter Eight: Around and About   60

Chapter Nine: Blackpool   75

Chapter Ten: Entertainment   85

Chapter Eleven: Stormy Weather   111

Chapter Twelve: Scouts and Guides   117

Chapter Thirteen: Churches Together   120

Chapter Fourteen: Shops and Businesses   124

Chapter Fifteen: From Dug-Out To Des Res   130

Chapter Sixteen: Past, Present and Future   136

ACKNOWLEDGEMENTS

Graham Baines, Mr D.H. Ball, Mrs Susan Donaldson, Norman Cooper, Helen and Chris Gleave, Carleton News, Carleton Pharmacy, Ian and Pauline Jackson, Mrs Joan Hart, Michael Loomes, Mrs Jean Parkinson, Ron Loomes, Mrs Barbara Strachan, Nicola Waring.

Old Fylde characters, from Knott End. Old Doilee (or Dolly) in the centre took in washing and also provided teas for visitors.

The Fylde countryside, between Poulton and Carleton, c. 1910.

INTRODUCTION

n today's world of changing values and shifting idealism, people thirst for tradition and knowledge of what used to be. With dismay we realise that a strange nebulous future of which we are half afraid is replacing a familiar past grafted into our beings. That which was once taken for granted, incorruptible and changeless, is now overshadowed. Alerted to losses we can ill afford, the average person eyes with despair the demolition of historic buildings, the passing of priceless treasure to other countries, old customs dying out, vandalism in all its forms, and terrorism.

The primal urge to trace ancestors has undergone a phenomenal upsurge in recent years; indeed, a sense of rootlessness is now acknowledged to be a factor in delinquency. Looking at the other side of the coin, however, it is cheering to realise that the human passage of local

1

history helps to shape word chronicles and that small communities like Carleton are a representative pattern of the nation's whole.

To wonder what our Carleton predecessors were like is endless fascination: how they amused themselves when bone-weary after a day's harvesting, or how they rested in the short evening that remained. How different were the long winters with the countryside hushed in snow, and icicles hanging on a frozen pump? How did they behave towards each other? What did they hope and strive for? Who lived in the house Aunt Jane inhabits, or tilled the land upon which your house is built?

Some of the answers, like pieces of a giant jigsaw idly flung, may be salvaged from the shipwreck of time; a pure seed-pearl of knowledge may suddenly illuminate what could previously not be explained. 'Who cares?' mutters the sceptic. Only the searcher knows the thrill of glimpsing that fellow-seeker who travelled centuries ago, making some contribution that has long outlived his modest span of years.

In this book I have tried to record some of the history of Great and Little Carleton - important events that shaped the communities in which we live, as well as the trivia and minutiae of everyday life -for the sake of future generations.

Chapter One
EARLY DAYS

The Elk

Relics of the past in the Carleton area don't get much older than the wonderful skeleton of a bull elk from twelve thousand years ago, known as the Highfurlong elk or Poulton elk. My feeling is that it would be better named were it called the Carleton Elk, as Carleton Moss would have been its extensive stamping ground. I also say Carleton because scanning the tithe map for field names such as Great Moss, North Ley Field, Smithy Field, Stack Yard Field and the proximity of Gazette Farm House (Gezzert's on earlier maps and in directories) rings Carleton bells.

Be that as it may, we have the vigilance of householder Mr A. Scholey to thank. He lived near the site which in 1970 was being prepared for house building. Mr Scholey knew the importance of keeping the bones wet and he alerted the Lancashire Record Office, a great help to the archaeologists who were called in to examine this wonderful discovery. It is now on permanent display at the Harris Museum in Preston.

Close examination of the elk's bones shows lesions, indicating that it had been hunted. Having sought escape, and being a swimming animal, this massive beast made for its favourite pool, managing, though injured, to evade its pursuers. There it died. In the chase a number of small, barbed arrows dropped from its body – and these were found nearby.

They provided more evidence for those who could correctly interpret the organic mud in which the carcase lay.

It should be said that since the discovery of this skeleton in 1970, being of such national importance, many interested parties have descended on the Harris Museum. Other theories have emerged, put forward by experts from the British Museum and the Natural History Museum. Minute drilling of a section of bone to bypass resin first used to preserve the skeleton has led to a closer dating, possibly 10,000 years ago.

Furthermore, *was* the animal hunted? Some damage to the skeleton could have been caused by bulldozers on the building site, at first unaware of the find. The small barbed arrows could not have produced fatal wounds. Could the frightened beast have crashed through an ice-covered pond and, under ice, been trapped, later to be preserved by another Ice Age? Were the small arrows used for fishing pike dropped by the hunters? We don't know.

Meanwhile Horace, as the elk is affectionately known, named I am told by Diane, Mr and Mrs Scholey's daughter, who was on the spot when the discovery was made, continues to fascinate, and I for one am happy to settle for that name and forego Carleton Elk.

From King Athelstan of Amounderness
After spending hours at Lancashire Record Office, peering at microfilms and leafing through bound volumes of newspapers over a hundred years old, it was finally borne in on me that Carleton must have been the original Sleepy Hollow, sandwiched between Blackpool, Fleetwood and Poulton-le-Fylde. Unlike residents from the latter townships, Carltonians, Great or Little (Magna or Parva as the old documents have it), apparently never got drunk and disorderly, were not brought up before Magistrate Giles Thornber for recovery of small debts, did not wheel barrow-loads on the pavement or speak rude words to the beadle. Page succeeds page, with never a mention of Carleton, except for the birth of a calf with five legs.

One of the earliest known documents including Carleton was the grant by King Athelstan of Amounderness to the Church of York on 7 June 934. Apart from Athelstan's document, the earliest original parchments I handled were the Shireburne of Stonyhurst papers, dated about 1230 and written in medieval Latin: 'This is the composition made

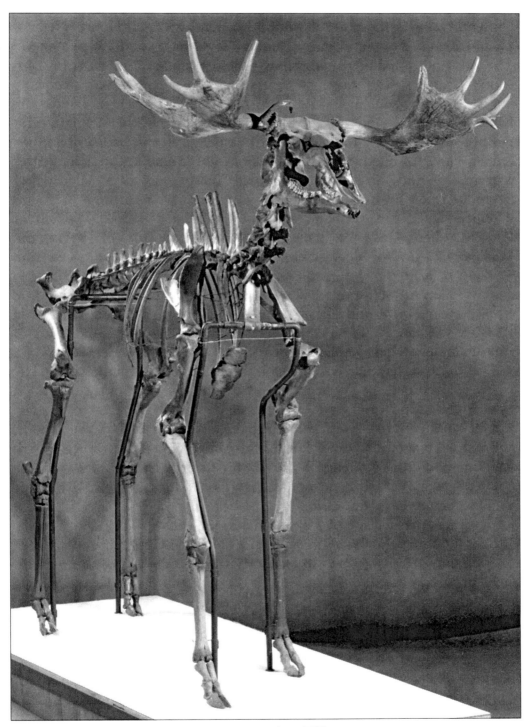

Horace the Elk.

between Geoffrey the prior and monks of Lancaster and Henry, priest of Wytington, concerning Henry's request to have a chapel at Karleton.' The prior and monks agreed. Henry could maintain a priest at his own expense, a priest who was to swear at the commencement of his ministry that he would maintain the rights of the mother church of Poulton-le-Fylde and claim none of the tithes and revenues belonging unless permitted to do so by the prior and monks and the vicar of Poulton. In return, Henry granted to prior and monks 'three shillings sterling' for his watermill of Karleton to be paid annually on the feast of St Michael, 29 September. Witnesses to this thirteenth-century agreement included 'Geoffrey the Crossbowman' and other influential names: William of Lathom, then Dean of Lancaster; Richard, Rector of Kyrkeham; William, Parson of Gayristang; Robert of Clachton; John, his son; William of Karleton; John, son of Walthelf of Pulton; Robert of Pulton and William of Thorneton. Obviously the hamlet of Karleton (the spelling changes over the years) was always influenced by landowners from Poulton, Garstang, Thornton and other areas of the Fylde, then part of Amounderness. There were, in those days, no Blackpool or Fleetwood.

Of old halls and families, mention within Carleton is fairly sparse. The place is recorded in William the Conqueror's Domesday Book as Carlentum, having 4 carucates of land under cultivation. A carucate or hide was the amount of land which could be ploughed in a year, using one plough, and support a family. These 4 ploughlands (another name for carucate) were held in the reign of Henry II by Baron Gilbert Fitz Reinfred. In the thirteenth century there is mention of Henry de Whittington, who had lands 'near Kokersand Abbey', giving 3 acres from the ville of Parva Carleton, formerly held by William de Pulton, Robert the ditcher and widow Matilda, to Stanlaw Abbey. At about the same time Henry de Carleton, son of Henry de Whittington, also granted to Stanlaw Abbey a right of way between his lands in Little Carleton and Staining. It is not easy to trace this descending footpath, but it began at Little Layton. Alongside this road, in return for the privilege of right of way, the monastery was to construct a ditch 7ft wide and 4ft deep, proof that flooding and drainage problems existed even at that time. Henry, son of Henry de Carleton, presented a large meadow, known as Ellercar, stretching as far as the Cecilie ditch in Little Layton, whose owner was Cecily de Layton. The use of the water collected in this ditch Henry wisely reserved for himself and his heirs, to turn the water-mill, and the monastery had to keep the ditch well scoured.

Richard the Demon of Poulton

We hear lots about witches, even in these technological days, wizards too, and for that we can perhaps blame Harry Potter, but how about demons? Poulton was not the only village to have one in the thirteenth century.

It was in 1276, during the reign of Edward I, the king who conquered Wales, when an excited crowd gathered where the Poulton market cross and stocks now stand. The chief men of the district, Carleton men among them, emerged from the Saxon moot hall, which was close to St Chad's Church and the tithe barn. With them was Sir Adam Banastre, a fiery tempered overlord who lived at Burn Hall close to the River Wyre, which later, a long time later, we knew as ICI (Imperial Chemical Industry). Geoffrey the Proctor and Adam the Reeve were also there but it was Richard the Demon who gave legality to the gathering. The Fylde was then known as the Hundred of Amounderness and Richard's title of 'Demon' or 'Demand' indicated great status. He was an official of the Hundred Court who could pronounce the judgement of that court – judgement then being known as 'doom'. The post was hereditary and included a grant of land. Demon as a title was in no way humorous, unlike the many nicknames bestowed in those early days – names such as Fathead, Longshanks, Eatbutter and Gatherpenny! It was a title bestowing dignity and still survives as Deemster, used for a judge in the Isle of Man, and Dempster, a name used in shipping.

The Hundred Court was of great importance, meeting at regular intervals. The jury was formed of freeholders.

Local landowners were also among the crowd: Richard de Brockholes, William de Thorneton and John Wenne. Feelings were running high as demands for tithes, rents and other dues made by the Prior of Lancaster were beyond a joke.

It had been arranged that the prior, Ralph de Truno, should meet the group assembled in what we now call Market Place and listen to their reasoning for a reduction of tithes and taxes, but the prior and his attendants were also in truculent mood. They not only refused to listen but they threatened the Poulton and Carleton men with dire consequences if they did not obey the demands of the Church. This infuriated our ancestors who had long suffered. Peasants and landowners rose in a body, overpowering the attendants and the prior himself. The quick-tempered Sir Adam Banastre ordered that the Church party, monks and prior, be carted off to Burn Hall where they were given a sound whipping. This, of course, was summary jurisdiction, overstepping the mark we might call it, and Richard the Demon could hardly condone taking the law into their own hands. It proved a salutary lesson, though. At the enquiry that followed, the prior and monks submitted to Adam's demands in order to get their release.

Richard the Demon pronounced judgement not entirely in favour of the prior, although the whippings were condemned. The prior was castigated for trespass. By crossing Adam de Banastre's land without

The site of Burn Hall, thought to be where the Battle of Brunaburgh took place.

permission he was caught on a point of law. The beginning of trial by jury had come in, under Common Law during Henry II's reign.

By the fourteenth century the title of Demon became 'le deman', Norman French) then 'le demand', but its meaning remained 'the man who pronounced dooms'.

It is interesting to note that the Leyland Hundred also had its demon, an official supported by land in Tarleton. In 1310 Robert Heppale of the lordship of Clitheroe held an enquiry and found that 'Walter le Demon did apply at the County Court of Lancaster for one oxgang of land [the amount of land that could be cultivated by one ox; it varied in size, according to soil quality] in Tarleton which he held of Robert by serjeantry', that is by fulfilling a public office instead of paying levies.

The meeting of the Leyland Hundred took place at Eccleston at the Cross Green and representatives from Bispham, Eccleston, Tarleton, Little and Much Hoole and Thorpe attended. They were armed with weapons and shook them to assert their rights, for they were all due for war levies. From this came the term 'wapentake'.

Roadside or 'Weeping' Crosses

At one time there were about five thousand 'weeping' roadside crosses in England, some of Saxon origin. Distances between villages and church were great, so funeral processions along the corpse roads halted by these roadside crosses to allow mourners to kneel, rest and pray. Think of these being around when Carleton and Poulton men fought at the battles of Flodden and Agincourt with 'Pilling men with pikes. Brought up on beef and bread', according to verse from those days.

The cross at Eccleston is interesting not only as it was the meeting place for the Hundred but also because it had a memorial inscription upon it to Walter the Demon. Poulton Cross may have been the rallying place for a similar display of weaponry. A mid-nineteenth-century cleric W.T. Bulpit, together with another historian, Henry Taylor, made a study of local history. Mr Bulpit was a curate at St Chad's, Poulton, and among much else he searched for the cross from Cross Green. (Eccleston had a second Green – the Village Green – where the Hundred meetings were held.) He and Mr Taylor found it in what had been a horse pond on the Green which had been filled up. They managed to restore and re-erect the stocks, but the cross had disappeared and all the demons with it in the relentless course of time.

In 1885 Henry Fishwick wrote a history of Poulton, in which he included information about roadside or 'weeping' crosses of which he said there were once many in Poulton, the oldest being Norcrosse or Nor-Cross. This was mentioned in a survey of the fourteenth century. He goes on to say: 'There was also a Northcrosse in Carleton, shown by a deed dated 29 April 1477 whereby Philip Bredkirk released to Richard Boteller a house and fifty acres of land in Northcrosse in the vil de Carleton which he had from James Pickering.' Vil is Norman French for township. Bredkirk and Boteller came down in later documents as the Bradkirk and Butler families.

(left) The cross in St Chad's churchyard, Poulton.

(below) This is all that remains of the ancient wayside cross in All Hallows' churchyard, Bispham.

Carletons and Sherburnes

The earliest reference to the Carleton family occurs in 1221 when Michael de Carleton paid a fine to Henry III because he had married Margaret Winwick without royal permission. Certainly the Carletons of Carleton were connected with the neighbourhood as lords of the manor for a very long time. William de Carleton's daughter Alicia married Sir Richard le Boteler of Rawcliffe Hall in 1281. Henry of Little Carleton and his wife Amabil granted an area then known as Hayholme to Henry le Boteler in 1283. Some of the Carletons fought with Henry V in France. Thomas Carleton held the manor till 1500; Lawrence Carleton was the last member of the family connected with the township, after which it passed to the Singletons. It was during the reign of Henry VIII that the Sherburnes of Stoneyhurst became owners of Carleton, acquiring the manorial rights and privileges later on. In 1717 Sir Nicholas Sherburne bequeathed the manor of Carleton to his only child and heiress Maria, the Duchess of Norfolk, who in turn left part of it to her relation Edward Weld of Lulworth Castle, Dorset. His descendant, Edward J. Weld, sold off the inheritance to small landowners. The Castle Gardens Inn was formerly known as the Weld Arms.

The Shireburn Rental

Dating from 1571, the Shireburn Rental is a crucial document from the Manor of Carleton which sheds much light on the community's early history. The rental and accounts were compiled for Sir Richard Shireburn and were studied in detail by W.F. Rea, whose findings were delivered in 1959 in *Transactions of the Historic Society of Lancashire and Cheshire*. Sir Richard was a Master Forester of Bowland and is described as energetic and self-assertive. In these rentals he refers to himself as steward and forester of Her Majesty's Forest of Amounderness. I have never seen any other reference to a Royal Forest in the Fylde and wonder when the land was deforested. Do any other documents referring to it survive, perhaps in the Public Record Office?

Sir Richard demolished his mansion, Stonyhurst Hall, and in its place commenced the imposing building which is now Stonyhurst College. Another striking monument to him is the fragile, beautiful bridge over the River Hodder known as Cromwell's Bridge. He joined with others to pay £70 and promised to provide the materials to build it. He had interests in the Fylde, the River Wyre being one, and in Hambleton, one of Carleton's 'near neighbours'. On 5 June 1572 he gave Nicholas Sumner £20 for 5 acres there (Holmclose) 'which brought in £1 13s 4d a year . . . for another acre and a half for which William Gaunt had to pay him a red rose, for ½ acre of meadow for which a red rose was also due and for a croft for which William Whiteside was to pay no rent at all'.

Many important local names appear in this document, usually listed as tenants. For Carleton there are Edward Bamber and Edward Bamber the elder, Edward Russell, William Davy, Robert Gilechristie, Wm Hoggarde, Thomas Gibson, Thomas Fletcher, Richard Hodgson, William Wright; for Norcross Wm Thorneton, John Haule, James Haule, Richard More, Henry Longmyre, James Warbryke, Wm Lawson, John Stephen, Wm Haull, Bailiff: John Holden. A few names appear

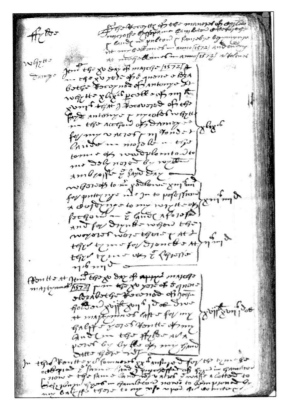

(left) A sample page from the Shireburn Rental of 1571.

(below) Hambleton Hall in the nineteenth century, when it was thatched.

incidentally in the later rentals – for Carleton in 1575 we find Ryc. Gylcryste, Willm Ambrosse, Henry Fissher, of Bispham (who had inherited from his grandfather, Wyllm); for Norcross in 1576 there is John Whiteside (his wife a daughter of Wm Lawson).

These were the only references to tenants. There is no detailed account of operations carried out – although the agent had organised gripping, ditching, ploughing, harrowing and harvesting and had bought 1500 quick-setts for hedging – an example of land reclamation and enclosure – on land which had been acquired in Hambleton.

It is worth noting that all the tenants listed had tenements as well as separate areas of land enclosed from Carleton Moor, so enclosure had been taking place there also.

I have also researched collections of title deeds and indentures deposited at the Lancashire Record Office which refer to Carleton. One indenture among deeds deposited by the *Lancashire Evening Post* is a lease of land in Little Carleton, husbandmen, dated 11 March 1694. The total acreage involved was estimated at 25 acres in four fields. The rent of South Hall Field was to be £12 10s 0d per annum and the other three fields together £30 per annum. The rent was to be paid on 2 February each year in the south porch of the parish church of Poulton. There was a penalty of £4 a year per acre if one of the 'closes' was ploughed up.

Among the thirty-two of Sir Richard's tenants in Carleton the name of Allen appears (Hugh and George Allen). George was the elder brother of Cardinal Allen and died in 1579 holding lands in Poulton, Norbreck and Thornton; he had also bought land in Hambleton from Nicholas Sumner.

Sir Richard had twenty-seven tenants in Hambleton who paid £21 a year for Shireburn Heyes, which was probably the site where present day Sherbourne Road was built. Sir Richard gave 2s in alms to the priest at Hamelton, as it was known in the sixteenth century. The church there dates from the Middle Ages and was surrounded by a moat; there is reference to 'a chamber lately builded in Hamelton and let to the priest of Hamelton.'

Carleton Hall and the Hole in the Wall
Of the two ancient buildings that would have intrigued us not a stone remains. Carleton Hall disappeared long ago but some ruins were visible in 1883 in a field opposite the farmhouse known as Gezzerts or

The early railway brochures referred to the 'typical Fylde peasant' – and here she is, at Quail Holme, Hackensall Woods, wearing sunbonnet and 'brat' as her ancestors had for centuries.

Gazzettes. Many have puzzled over the name but I favour an explanation linked to the old word Guisarts, which refers to being disguised or wearing masquerade dresses for Christmas revelry and mumming. It is likely that such a group gathered at Gezzerts farm on the outskirts, dressing up there before going the rounds of Great and Little Carleton. October 1592 shows the last mention of Carleton Hall in the registers, when a man called Thomas Kellet was buried from there. Another vanished building, a beerhouse known as the Hole in the Wall, housed a manorial court. Twelve jurymen with other officers had the duties of inspecting hedges, ditches and watercourses and passing judgement on people who had neglected them.

The manorial court was moved from the Hole in the Wall to the Weld Arms but sessions fell into disuse when the estate, along with Norcross Farm, was sold. There were people in Carleton in 1885 who could recall not only this but also the use of the ducking-stool or cuckstool in Great Carleton. The pond, now drained, is opposite Leach's Farm.

Thornton Hall, similar perhaps to Carleton Hall, is seen here in 1951 when the house and farm were owned by Mr Silcock.

A typical blacksmith's shop, this one near Scotforth.

Handling the will of the Dowager Duchess of Norfolk, a document dated 19 February 1745, was interesting but tantalising: interesting in its further partitioning of the land, its naming of local gentry (for example 'Fleetwood Hesketh, son of Roger Hesketh of Rossall'; '. . . Tulketh House, Preston'), and conditions laid down about the grinding of corn. Such references as 'gardens, barns, stables, orchards, buildings – farmers and tenants together with all and singular houses' tease the researcher.

So it is to the apportionment in lieu of tithes, the tithe awards and plans (begun at Carleton in 1838) and to the various censuses that one has to turn for place, time and fact.

Tithes and Censuses

Four Lane Ends, Carleton, comprising the crossroads formed by the junction of the old roads from Great Carleton to Thornton (B5258) and from Poulton to Bispham (A5267) has, since the last century, been known as 'Town End' or 'Four Lane Ends within Carelton' or 'Lane Ends'. Anyone who has walked or cycled along the Bispham Road will appreciate its age. Persistently meandering curves, very dangerous to modern traffic, suggest its original use as a drovers' road when cattle would habitually graze by the wayside on the lushest grass, thus flattening this winding road at their whim to be followed by man ever since. With school, inn and smithy in close proximity, Four Lane Ends, apart from additions and styles of buildings, has altered appreciably little and is the hub of Carleton. A closer look at the villagers who lived thereabouts breathes life into statistics, and helps us to become better acquainted with neighbours who lived over a hundred years ago, for people are the stuff of history and make the latter come alive.

Collecting tithes was a system bred from monastic times. The Benedictine Order, strong agriculturists, wanted a tenth of what the land produced. Not only was it difficult to collect a tenth sheaf of corn, a tenth pig, sheep or cow, even a tenth pail of milk, it was hopeless in large parishes and a headache to the farmer because he could not legally remove his crops until the tithe owner had taken his share. This could be disastrous if there was delay. Frustration forced many to make money agreements. One tithe reformer in the Fylde claimed, 'I don't get much more than a fourth part of my dues. If I collected my tithes in kind I would be harassed to death by the landowners.' Before the end of the eighteenth century most tithes had been unofficially converted. Thomas Greene of Lancaster introduced the first bill to commute tithes in 1828. Nearby Cockerham had settled disputes by private Acts of Parliament as early as 1824. Coinciding with a general decline in agriculture, the 1836 Tithe Commutation Act was timely, supported by the 1846 Amendment Act which ironed out any remaining difficulties. Carleton's Award is dated 1839 and a map and schedule is kept at the Lancashire Record Office. So it was that a fixed annual payment, far more convenient, was arrived at by unbiased assessors like John Job Rawlinson, barrister at law, one of many appointed as an assistant tithe commissioner. Very detailed maps showing buildings, dwellings and fields (all numbered) linked up with schedules giving field names, owners, occupiers, acreage, use of land and the sum payable in lieu. The assessors had to spend a long time in the district to cover such detail and these records are now invaluable to the researcher.

Decisions were as follows: 'One shilling is payable for every acre of hay grass mown of the ancient Lancashire measure of seven yards to the perch, instead of the tithes of hay in kind; one penny for every milk cow instead of the tithe of her milk; halfpence for every calf instead of the tithe of foals; and one penny for every hive of bees instead of the tithes of honey and swarms; one halfpenny is payable for every Inhabitant Householder instead of the tithes of eggs and chickens.' It is interesting to note that in our area Sir Peter Hesketh Fleetwood generously relinquished his rights to 'the great tithes of wool and lamb'. The Tithe Award Map of 1838 of Four Lane Ends, Carleton, reveals some delightful names: Old Woman's Field, Great Moor Hey, Higher Mill Field, Ley Field, Jenny's Field, Old Meadow, Little School Field, Holden's Field, Kate's Field. It shows the windmill, the familiar bends in the roads, all backed by the Schedules which go into more interesting detail:

1   Number 274 Old Meadow was owned and occupied by Richard and Betty Dewhurst who also owned and occupied 336 Kate's Field.

2   334 Weld's Meadow was owned by Joseph Weld but occupied by John Brining (the latter had a watching brief over the Overseers of the Poor for Carleton).

3   Joseph Weld's Stockyard, Calf Croft House and outbuilding,

garden, barn, meadow and Little Whinney Field (345–51) were all in the use of John Brining, further proving him to be a man of substance and local influence.

4   Cottage, garden, barn and Ley Field, John Brining owned and occupied.

5   Robert Haslam, who has descendants living in Haslingden today, worked Weld's Old Woman's Field and East Old Woman's Field, Long Moor Hey and two gardens.

6   Thurston Haslam, son of Robert, owned cottages and garden 364. The Census of 1841 reveals the Haslams as a large family involved in the butchery trade.

The census enumerators' returns of 1841, taken on 31 March, were the first full-scale detailed British census and, especially when scanned in relation to tithe awards, the Carleton section is full of human interest. Questionnaires were distributed to each household. This information was recorded in the census enumerator's book for the township. This first census, although marred by vagueness of addresses and lack of detailed information, does reveal the largeness of families. Recording commenced at Holm Nook, Holm, Norcross, Whitholme proceeding to New Ryscar and Old Ryscar. Families to the north of Four Lane Ends include the Brinings at Rington, the Porters towards Four Lane Ends, the Bagots, numbering five (agriculture), and the Haslams, numbering ten (butcher). One child of the six Haslam children, Robert, was apprenticed as a joiner. The Cartmells were a family of nine, the youngest being one month old. There were seven Cleggs (shoemaker and clogger) and fourteen Hardmans, their youngest being two-year-old James. One wonders if they successfully fed all those mouths while father pursued the trade of wheelwright. The Carter family, amounting to seven, were supported by William, aged forty-five, an agricultural labourer. Well-to-do farmer John Brining had a household of nine and could hire agricultural help and female servants. Thomas Brining, John's older brother, was farming at Rington in 1841. The human interest divulged is infinite.

Ninety individuals were spread over eighteen households and the occupations in this small community included cooper, miller, blacksmith, ropemaker, carrier, butcher, mantua maker, publican, farmer and joiner. These are echoes from a past world that has ceased to be, but the picture of an agricultural community emerges. A quick survey of the 1851 Census with its greater detail reveals some interesting changes in Carleton. Miles Shaw of Bridge End, has invested in property. The Cartmells are now at Ossa Mill. Another blacksmith, residing at Forshaw's Hill, has become necessary to deal with more horses. Richard Cumming is farming the 14 acres of Gezarts, while Robert Poole tackles the 57 acres of Scut House, Highfurlong, that ancient dwelling on the old road to the coast. Throughout the whole of the district of Fylde an increase of 1,131 in population has taken place in ten years:

10,751 males in Fylde
11,154 females in Fylde
3,926 inhabited houses
212 uninhabited houses
35 houses in course of erection

In Carleton the increase in population was a mere twenty-three.

Hackensall Hall, one of the many ancient Fylde manor houses.

Lizzie Parkinson churning butter. (Norman Cooper)

Chapter Two
FYLDE FAMILIES

Bambers, Shaws and Parkinsons

Certain names crop up again and again in the Carleton area, as we have already seen. As early as 1598 there is a reference in the parish registers to the birth of a daughter Margaret to John Bamber of Carleton. Bambers of the Moor in Carleton were residents in the seventeenth century, the death of one James being recorded in May 1617. He was buried at Poulton, which also had 'a great moor land', the latter in the area now called Moorland Road. Roger Sherburne was his father-in-law and in his will, Jenet his wife is bequeathed Moor House. The brother of James was Richard, among whose eight children was Edward 'The priest of Carleton', who is thought to have been executed at Lancaster in 1646, bravely standing by his religious beliefs. After the Bambers left the Moor it became the home of Richard Singleton. The Shaws of Bridge End, Carleton, were one branch of a numerous Fylde family. John Shaw (1819–76) lived there. George Shaw, 'Vicar of Poulton', is included in the Hearth Tax returns for Poulton in 1666 when the vicarage was assessed at four hearths. Married twice, his second wife was Margaret Bamber of the 'Moor'. In 1851 Miles Shaw owned Bridge End.

Of the Parkinson family, widely represented in the Fylde, Richard, born 1793, had a business in Poulton. There were members of the family in Poulton, Little Poulton, Carleton, Marton, Newton, Thornton and

Holmes. The will of Richard Parkinson of Risecar ('old Riscow'), Great Carleton, was proved in 1809 and there was a Richard Parkinson residing in Carleton in the eighteenth century who had two sons, Thomas (born 1761) and Richard (born 1763).

One must touch here on the famed longevity of Fylde residents. Mrs Margaret Croft's death at the age of ninety-two was reported in the *Fleetwood Chronicle* on 11 October 1845. She left two brothers, William Parkinson of Carleton, aged ninety-four, and James Parkinson of Garstang, aged ninety-six.

During the reign of Elizabeth I James Massey of Carleton built the mansion of Whinneis or Whinney Heys, derived from Whin, the country name for gorse. This area, yellow with gorse – the site is near the present Victoria Hospital – stretched as far as Carleton. Occasional small woods indicated sites of the remnants of ancient peat bogs. Married to John Foyle in the eighteenth century, Susannah Veale, born at Whinney Heys, was also a resident of Bridge End, at about the time when Squire Thomas Tyldesley was galloping between the more important residences, forever calling in, hungry and thirsty.

Polly and Agnes Parkinson, Carleton sisters, c. 1890. (Norman Cooper)

Polly, Agnes and Ernest Parkinson, a few years later. (Norman Cooper)

Nellie Parkinson's General Store and Post Office on Poulton Road, Carleton, looking towards Poulton, c. 1870. Under a magnifying glass it is possible to see three children standing near the tree, and a long-gowned lady at the door of the shop, possibly Nellie herself. The shop was never open on a Sunday, when the bull's eye glass window and door were shrouded with a thick blind. Nellie eventually had to move into a terraced house opposite this typical Fylde cottage, which must have been constructed over 300 years ago and was knocked down in the mid-twentieth century. (Mr D.H. Ball)

THE STOCKS
POULTON-LE-FYLDE.

The stocks, Poulton. James Danson (1852–1906) is the merry bearded figure on the left. This is the only photograph of him that survives.

The Dansons of Carleton

The cheery face of bearded James Danson larking about in Poulton Stocks, amusing passers-by in the late nineteenth century, set Susan Donaldson on tracing family trees – and a good job she made of her research, uncovering some interesting facts about Great and Little Carleton and thereabouts. James was her great-grandfather.

James was born in 1852 at Trap Farm, son of Henry Danson, yeoman, and Elizabeth Calvert of Upper Rawcliffe. Through census returns it became clear that he was one of six sisters and three brothers. The sisters married familiar Fylde names Cookson, Gaulter, Brownhill and Cardwell.

Susan traced the family back to John Danson, baptised in 1736, son of Peter Danson, husbandman of Thornton. John Danson's will was drawn up at Holmenook and his daughter Jennet married John Bryning.

By the 1851 Census there were thirteen people living at Trap Farm, Carleton, the Danson family and two servants – a severe case of overcrowding.

At the time of the stocks photograph James had moved to Potts Alley, off Market Place, Poulton, now renamed Chapel Walks, a mews of nice shops and a café. As Potts Alley, on the site of the old Parkinson's

Trap Farm was home to the Danson family. The cruck-framed farmhouse would originally have been thatched. (Susan Donaldson)

Corn Mill, it was far less salubrious, indeed notorious, as lodging houses for sailors – when Poulton was still a port and had thirteen inns.

The Brinings

Links between the Danson family and the Brining family came about when John Brining married Jennet Danson on 23 September 1786. Their marriage bond is recorded at the Lancashire Record Office. As an alternative to having the banns of marriage read, such licences or 'dispensations' could enable a marriage to take place at any time and at any place; this was more expensive so not as popular. Some couples had both banns and 'dispensation', perhaps on the bride's insistence.

Further proof, to protect the Church from performing illegal marriages, was by the swearing of an affidavit. 'Know all men by these present that we John Brining and Henry Danson of Carleton, in the parish of Poulton are held and firmly bound in £200 of good and lawful money of Great Britain to be paid to the Right Reverend Father and settled with our seals.'

John Brining, described as husbandman, and Jennet Danson of

Carleton were both twenty-one years old and their marriage was solemnised at Poulton parish church, witnesses being John's brother and Prudence Jackson, a friend. John Brining senior, who had married in the same church on 21 October 1761, had a prominent role in Carleton, being responsible for the Day Book of Carleton's money.

Mrs Donaldson's research goes on to prove that there were five children born of John and Jennet's marriage, between 1762 and 1772, but sadly the children Richard and Jane had died within three weeks of each other and their mother Jennet died aged only thirty-nine, but John the father lived on until the age of seventy-eight in 1820. Sons John and Thomas had large families that proved to be long living, but not all got married.

The custom persisted of naming members after their forebears, a trial to the historian! In my family it was Edward William and William Edward that were seemingly used alternately for eldest sons of eldest sons.

The 1841 Census reveals that some of the Brining family were living at Rington Farm, Carleton, of whom daughter Peggy married John Walsh of Marsh Farm. Elsewhere in the book John is highlighted as the first in the district to successfully experiment with guano manure. In the 1861 Census John Walsh is shown as farming 144 acres with a staff of eight. He and John Brining were well known in Carleton. John Brining occupied Weld's Meadow – Weld's stockyard, Calf Croft House with outbuilding, barn meadow and little Whitney Field all being under his control.

John Brining, man of substance and of much local influence, went on to own and occupy 'cottage, barn and Lay Field'. What is more, he lived to be ninety-two and spent retirement at 2 Dick's Mill, Carleton.

Rington Farm, Carleton. Quite recently the farmhouse was refurbished, but land sold to Faircloughs Builders has now been covered with modern houses. The rural scene has been transformed. (Joan Hart)

Chapter Three
DAILY LIFE

Memories

Miss Mary Alice Penswick, born in 1894, and Miss Alice Jane Livesey had strong memories of the good fare they received as children: on Sundays a big joint of beef, all kinds of vegetables, mint sauce, potatoes, bacon all year, hams in the summer, rice puddings and black jacks (muscatel raisins in steamed pudding), sausage, liver and onions, hash or 'scouse'. Pies arrived in season – rhubarb, gooseberry, red currant, white currant, plums, damson, raspberry and 'beautiful prune pie'. Bread was baked twice a week. At Nellie Parkinson's shop butter, lard, treacle and flour were sold loose and the flour bin stood alongside the paraffin drum. It was a time of good food and good fires in the grate, for everything was done by the fire, which warmed bodies, water and the oven. A strong fireguard at the Liveseys, made by the blacksmith from Old Kilshaw's Farm, kept the children safe from accidents. The fire blazed, sparkling the brasswork of the 'Tidy Betty' (fire irons) and fender, gleaming from the frequent polishing they received. Black-leaded, with trim rubbed bright by using fine emery paper, the family fire-grate was welcoming for everyone to sit round and it aired the clothing spread over their heads on a clothes rack, operated by a pulley which hoisted to ceiling height.

The Livesey family in the back garden of their house in Croasdale terrace, Carleton, c. 1900. The children are Alice Jane, Catherine Mermet (better known as Kate), Annie and their brother Thomas Seiah.

One of Alice Jane's vivid childhood memories was visiting the smithy and helping to blow the bellows. She could recall the smell of the hot metal shoe being clamped to the hoof of a heavy shire horse. The smith made other metal items besides their fireguard: gates and farm implements and the iron hoops which had to be skilfully clamped round large wooden cart wheels. Two men with long irons lifted the hot metal circle and put it onto the wheel complete with its hub and spokes.

Miss Livesey worked for a while at Kilshaw's, collecting eggs, accompanied by Lady, a dog who was an excellent ratter. From there she went on to the art of cheese making at Garstang, at first by hand – using a barrel with a lid and handle. The whey was run off, the handle turned, and curds allowed to set in a mould under a press. Covered with muslin cloth and oiled, this traditional Lancashire cheese was ready for sale in a fortnight. Butter made from the whey was very good, but sometimes this went for pig food or was given away.

Pinafores and sun bonnets protected hair and clothing, the latter being usually of linsey-woolsey, a white or red homespun flannel for the girls – there was once a factory at Bispham that made this cloth. The men and boys wore thick, rough shirts of the same material, moleskin trousers and clogs. 'Monkey' clogs were for Sunday best. Housewives wore a 'brat' or apron, but at holiday times and for church out came the finery. Winter fashions offered by Mr R. Warbrick at Fleetwood were made of fine broad and narrow cloths, cashmeres and Scotch linens sold at 5½d a yard, Gingham at 4d a yard, Mousline-de-laine dresses for 10s 6d sale price. Men's moleskins could be bought for 15s, boys' corduroy suits for 5s, and there were large assortments of carpet bags, leather hat cases, woollen scarfs, wool Guernseys, stocks, fronts, collars, hats and caps at what seem very low prices. Fifty pieces for patchwork – print, plush, silk – could be had for 10d if you were making a quilt, and a Jones new hand sewing machine, beautifully enamelled and ornamented with gold, could be bought for 4 guineas in May 1873.

Remedies were mainly home-made. Neighbours served as midwives and Doctor Anderson was not called out unless absolutely necessary. Sulpholine lotion was advertised locally as curing skin disease; Dr King's

Old or Lower Kilshaw's Farm, Poulton Road, Carleton. A wheelwright's shop and a smithy used to be attached to this eighteenth-century house, but they were demolished when the new Kilshaw's Farm was built behind the old.

dandelion and quinine pills 'purified the blood, soothed the liver, stomach and bowels'. Cockle's Pills, Dr De Roos' Vegetable Life Drops, Apple Butter and Powell's Balsam of Aniseed were all available in the 1880s along with wonderful cures for baldness and, be it known, 'Teeth supplied by Mr G.H. Jones, Surgeon Dentist, have obtained prize medals in London, Paris, Vienna, New York and Berlin . . . they render mastication and articulation excellent'. He must have ousted Mr Richeraud who was visiting Southport, Blackpool, Poulton and Fleetwood as early as 1845 and charging 2s 6d for a filling, 5s for restoring teeth to beautiful colour and 5 guineas for a full set of false teeth; 'mineral teeth fixed from one to a complete set in a style not to be surpassed'. Richeraud's celebrated tooth powder, he declared, was patronised by the Royal Family.

Herb teas for tranquillising effects were made from angelica, lemon balm, chamomile, feverfew, hops, lavender, marjoram, mint, sarsasparilla and rosemary. Herbs are coming into their own again in the modern world.

The visit of the hurdy gurdy man once a year to Carleton was looked forward to. He did his rounds using a hand cart, a small monkey with a large appetite accompanying him. Trapp Farm was where they stayed for a few days before moving on, their itinerary covering the whole of the Fylde.

Chapter Four
CARLETON PARISH

The Day Book of 1787

Going back two centuries into Carleton archives, one of the most interesting and human documents dealing with the parish is the 'Day Book or particular account of the Town's Money laid out from April 24th 1787 by me John Clarkson, the hired Overseer of the Poor under Paul Harrison and John Brining'. Examples of entries from this and from subsequent years are as follows:

1786 Molly Harrison paid to her for the 27th April to 28th September 22 weeks £2 4s 0d. October 19th paid towards her son a shirt 1s

1791 paid to John Brining for half a load of meal 14s

1794 paid Richard Green for delving and fencing Silcock's and Southworth's gardens 8 days at 10s 8d

a quire of paper 1s 3d

making land tax and Window assessment 7s

going to Poulton to consult with lawyer Hull, expences 1s

going to Preston with Land tax 7s 6d

paying the High Constable 6d

paid for paper to make militia lists 2d

Bidding and attending funerals, making the lists of ages

coffin £1
bread 1s 8d
sugar 4d

Expences. Little Side:
moles £4 18s 6d
pinfold gate and stoop 20s
(Great Side also had problems with moles for in 1823 'moles
catching' cost 15s 9¾d)
paid for waiscotts 3s
paid Brindle workhouse £1 4s 6d
Fire for Towne's House at Great Carleton to John Sanderson for a
load of turfe 12s 9d
Thomas Smith for fetching 36 baskets of coales 9s
Margaret Dixon 2 shifts 6s 6d
a petty coat 6s 6d
bed gown 4s 5d
paid for shifting her to Molly Harrison's 1s

The poor must indeed have felt they were a burden on the parish.

Disease
Bad sanitary conditions led to outbreaks of fevers in spite of the healthy
country and sea air. Undrained low-lying areas of the Fylde were
particularly dangerous, and at Carleton in 1892 a catastrophe of such
proportions occurred that it had to be officially investigated. Doctor
Maclean Wilson's Report to the Local Government Board on an enquiry
into 'a very fatal outbreak of diphtheria at Breedy Butts Farm in the
Fylde Rural Sanitary district' disclosed that from a family of thirteen, nine
were attacked with the disease and seven died. The report on Breedy
Butts, an area of boulder clay at the edge of a flat carr, revealed appalling
sanitary conditions: 'ditches dirty with sewage' . . . 'five feet from the
pump well is a cess pool made from an old petroleum barrel half-full of
semi-solid filth . . . trapped gullies . . . a blocked drain which passes
through the farmyard. Diphtheria is endemic in this part of Lancashire
and since 1875 and has only been absent or unnoticed one year.' Doctors
Winn, Williams and Anderson, the three medical men in the area, had
wide experience of this disease, as well as mumps and scarlet fever.

'There has apparently been frequent occurrence of wholesale destruction of a family by epidemic disease in the district.'

In 1901 the joint Sewerage Committee had plenty to talk about. It was revealed that conditions in Robin's Lane, if allowed to remain, 'would in hot weather become a veritable death trap', but no immediate action was taken. However, the first sewers, part of a joint scheme for Thornton, Bispham and Carleton, were sanctioned by the Local Government Board on 2 May 1902.

Parish Councillors

A meeting held in the schoolroom attracted seventy people on 4 December 1894 and was for the purpose of electing parish councillors. It was a simply done business: each candidate had to put himself forward and prove his worth, and there was then a show of hands. William Jemson and Ralph Passe, the latter of Carleton Villa, were present at the meeting as Overseers of the Poor. Candidates were Richard Bibby of Moor Farm; Charles Butler, butcher; Robert Hodgkinson, farmer and carter of Carleton; William Longbottom, restaurant keeper of Carleton Cottage; William Nelson, manager for Norcross Farm; John Parkinson, grocer and carter, of Carleton; John T.H. Taylor of Bridge End farm; and William Wade of Randell's farm, Carleton. These nominees were questioned and all expressed their views – some better than others. Mr Bibby wanted gas, a library and wash houses for Carleton but remarked that 'a good bath could be had in the sea'. William Nelson received thirty votes, Richard Bibby twenty-eight, William Longbottom, 'who had done his best on the Burial Board and would do his best for the township', received only four votes and was not elected.

Roads

The bad state of the highways was debated at a meeting on 4 March 1901, which desired a portion of the township to be lighted up from Poulton boundary to Four Lane Ends, Carleton.

A very interesting report dated 1928 lists the roads in Carleton under the Fylde Rural District Council, revealing names which have vanished: Rhodesia, Wreawood, Stocks Lane, Primrose Hill. Improvements needed were to the 'hairpin bend between Higham House and Bridge End Farm, the bend at Dick's Mill and the removal of the manure heap on the road near Higher Moor Farm'. Reporting on field footpaths and

Cows coming in for milking, Poulton Road, c. 1909. (Norman Cooper)

stiles, swing gates needed repairing, planks across ditches replacing and 'a footpath had been ploughed up'. One wonders how many ancient rights of way have been lost.

A Carleton Directory of 1924

Barretts Directory of Fylde and District describes Carleton thus: 'Carleton adjoins Poulton on the west and is the parliamentary division of the Fylde county council, and is part of the Fylde Union. The parish council consists of seven members. The township contains 1,786 acres and its rateable value is £14,065.'

Carleton's steady population growth is recorded: 1861: 363; 1871: 433; 1881: 441; 1891: 417; 1901: 684; 1921: 959.

At this time the parish council consisted of James Beaver (chairman), William Barritt, Sam Briggs, H. Carr, John Brown, J. Fielding and J. Sanderson.

We had a good postal service in those days. Letters arrived at John Parkinson's shop at 6.30am and 5.30pm and they were delivered at 8.50am and 7.30pm respectively.

Mr Fielding, a distant relation, lived at Romleigh. Delectable house names like Clovelly, Avondale, Hawthorn Cottage, Holm Eden, Red

Lea, Willow Bank, Fairbourne. Dingleside and Milbourne House starred Carleton's letters, and there was no need to add street names at all – or if you did, just the street sufficed. I have frequently wondered what Mr Amaziah Greaves of The Limes was interested in. He was not a farmer. And where were Rose Villa and Primrose Bank situated? One must presume the dwellings had a name change or were simply swept away in the press of time, for some of the cottages would still have been thatched at this time, having been built in the sixteenth and seventeenth centuries.

A count of farmers in 1924 numbers thirty-seven. Examples are Edin Hardman who was at Scut House, John James at Trapps Farm, Richard Penswick at Gazette Farm, Thomas Strickland at Ryscarr, and William Pye at Carleton Lodge.

Union, UDC and Borough

Carleton was one of the twenty-four townships in the Fylde Union. By 1921 the population of the Union had reached 170,265 and covered an area of 67,509 acres, the area of Carleton being 1,786 acres, population 959, value £10,892. In 1868 H. Billsborrow was one of the guardians; in 1929 J. Fielding, both of Carleton. The Chairman of the Fylde Union in 1929 was William Hodgson, who devoted his life to the service of the community and lived at The Sycamores, Poulton-le-Fylde (opposite the library). He was the first Chairman of the Urban District Council. By the 1930s Blackpool wanted to amalgamate with the ancient market town of Poulton, but the Urban District Council wished to remain aloof and increased in size by attaching part of Carleton, Hardhorn and Singleton. In 1974 the Local Government Act saw further changes, with Carleton and Poulton becoming part of the new Borough of Wyre.

Chapter Five
FARMS AND FARMERS

Old maps, directories and documents prove Carleton to have been a dedicated farming community and up to recent years this continued to be so. In ancient days the River Wyre side of Thornton was a swamp constantly covered by tide as far as Burn Naze, the area being named Bergerode. The marsh at Thornton, which joined part of Carleton, was a wild common with very few farms, but it was acknowledged that 'the rich land along this coast was that including Bispham village, Warbreck, Carleton, Layton, Poulton, Hardhorn and Staining'. Some of the farms were very old. Prospect Farm had a plaque dated 1670 and Thomas Tyldesley's diary from 1712–14 shows them to have been of long standing even then. This squire's jottings reveal the round of seasons, referring to fishing, hunting, cock-fighting, ploughing, sowing, hay-making. 'All day very bussy in my hay and in the evening cleared the Bryory Field . . . gott a boat load of terfe into my seller'. An Enclosure Act on 13 June 1799 divided, allotted and enclosed Thornton Marsh. Carleton Marsh, situated on the coast between Bispham and Carleton, was reclaimed in about 1800.

John Walsh of Marsh Farm was the first to experiment with guano manure, and the results very much interested Bold Fleetwood Hesketh, Lord of the Manor. The news had reached Carleton, with its thirty or so farms, that ships had travelled to the island of faraway Ichaboe and were

Rowing for potatoes, Breedy Butts Farm, Carleton, c. 1903.

queuing up to collect the deposits of guano as trade was poor and agriculture at a low ebb. John spread 28lb of guano on one-sixteenth of an acre before it was ploughed, then sowed it with beans. Whereas the guano-treated area cropped 294lb of beans and 388lb of straw and chaff, a similar piece without guano resulted in a yield of only 178lb of beans and 240lb of straw and chaff.

There was a tremendous interest in agricultural machinery and the farm lads would tramp miles on a Sunday, comparing results at neighbouring farms. A public trial of mowing machines in a field at Norcross was held on 12 June 1868 when Mr Eden, agent for farming implements, supplied machinery to demonstrate on James Fairclough's land which had a luxuriant crop of clover and rye grass. 'Horses were lent and driven by Thomas Walsh of Thornton, John Foster of Carleton, and Cuthbert Fair of Norcross. All the machines tested were bought there on the spot and the crowd dispersed at 4 o'clock.' It was the year following bread riots, the setting up of soup kitchens, the Sultan of Turkey's visit to England and the winter when forty people drowned by falling through the ice in Regent's Park.

Declining farming in 1896 led to big sales, which show how much equipment and valuable breeding stock were held in the Carleton area. Farm implements included 'Seven-horse-power thrashing machine by Marshall, First Class Corn Mill, Hay Cutter, Market carts with patent

Haymaking at Bankes Farm, Carleton, c.1900. Mr Graham is on the left, Jim Parkinson on the top of the haycart and Ernest Parkinson on the right. (Norman Cooper)

gearing, jobbing carts, Market traps, milk floats, 3 set Diamond harrows, 2 Scarifiers, 3 Swing ploughs, sheep dipping troughs', and scores of other items. Similarly the sale of Rowlands Farm lists valuable horses with their pedigrees, prize-bred Golden Wyandotte poultry, Toulouse geese and Rouen ducks and drakes together with all manner of dairy utensils and farm equipment.

Much was expected of the tenant and a bad year could ruin. Under the terms for letting a farm at £18 per year payable on 5 June, a tenant in the early nineteenth century was not allowed to 'set any more potatoes in any one year than shall be absolutely necessary for the consumption of himself and family . . . a tenant must not plow, dig, delve, break up or convert with tillage . . . any other part of the fields and if he does he shall pay to the landlord £20 an acre'.

Carleton very successfully ran a Cow Club to which all the farmers contributed and should one member lose a cow he was paid £8. George Hutchinson of Breck Street, Poulton, was the nearest veterinary surgeon, but many farmers tried their own cures, for example Arthur Rowbotham's receipt for foul in the foot (yellow resin, turpentine, mutton fat and a pint of train oil). The farmers' wives also had their own ideas and preferences. Water brought from the Holy Well at Hardhorn, for instance, was especially good for butter making. A cross or a horseshoe was often nailed to the dairy or buttery, and a stone with a hole in the centre tied to the door could prevent milk turning sour, long thought to be the work of witches.

Ryescar Farm, Carleton, c. 1980.

Carleton featured in a Blackpool and Fylde District Agricultural Show towards the end of the nineteenth century when 'fifty horses brought from Carleton, bred by the tenantry of the district' were sold at Bailey's Hotel. One resident recalls how good natured the farmers were especially in their concern for horses. When people moved house their belongings would be pulled on carts and if it were a long distance, people and horses were allowed to put up in the barns overnight. When the farmer himself moved he would take his livestock 'on the hoof'.

Old residents, familiar with a farming community and its ways, stress 'nature's way' in animal husbandry and rotation of crops. Calves and lambs were born in spring when the fresh grass was growing. Hens were allowed to roost in the trees in winter until they began to lay again. In 1771 Arthur Young reported on Lancashire's cropping rotation: winter corn, spring corn, pasture. One hundred years later the same system was still being observed in Carleton.

Wildfowl shooting in the snow, possibly at Orchard Farm, Carleton Marsh, c. 1870.

'Owd England', a Norbreck fisherman, c. 1870.

Chapter Six
WINDMILLS

Dick's Mill

t seems a rare compliment that even after a hundred years a minor landmark should be affectionately referred to by the Christian name of one of its tenants, Richard Baron, whose family had such a great reputation for the fine grade of flour they produced at Hambleton peg mill. At one time he was the miller at Poulton Mill, as some maps named it – although it was referred to by the locals as Dick's Mill, and the informal name stuck.

Situated at the acute bend of the road beyond Four Lane Ends past what was once Carleton Post Office (also a grocer's shop), it was originally a brick tower mill with the interior reducing in width as each storey was ascended. From basement to top were open steps like a ladder with no handrail. 'You steady yourself by a rope suspended all along the stairs from the top of the mill to the bottom,' said Allen Clarke when he visited. For a short time it was driven by steam until in a great Fylde gale one day the sails whirled themselves dizzy, going quite mad until the gearing broke and they eventually split, flying off in all directions. The building shuddered into a heap of bricks but fortunately no one was hurt. It lay, a forlorn ruin, until a Carleton man bought it and, using the bricks, built three cottages – some indication of how strongly made were the walls of tower mills. The old millstones were at one time in the back yard of the landlord's house in the next row, but have now disappeared.

Today's residents living on the site of Dick's Mill are very much aware of its history, and I was shown the last relics in what was Mr and Mrs Bridge's back garden. These appear to be a quern or a post socket and a small, moss-grown, circular stone once part of the windmill's mechanism. The datestone incorporated into one of the cottages shows that the builder was loath to forget Dick. Looking up between two bedroom windows it is still possible to see this stone, carved in relief with a windmill and the words 'Dick's Mill Terrace A.D. 1880'. But look again at the stone, now so worn that the last digit looks like 0; originally that was 6 – and research shows that the Terrace was erected in 1886. Wind and weather are sweeping away the whole inscription.

The sign above Dick's Mill Terrace.

Dick's Mill is number 367 on the Tithe Schedules. John Kirkham operated the mill in 1841 with the usual malt kiln and yard attached but he does not appear to have lived here. He owned cottages close by which were occupied by James Barnes, described as 'miller' – so he was probably employed by Kirkham.

Opposite Dick's Mill, Edmund Thornton senior and junior carried on their trade as blacksmiths. Their cottage was extended in later years

The Mill House, rebuilt with bricks that came from Dick's Mill. (Barbara Strachan)

and by 1861 was known as Thornton Villas, a row still standing on what must be the most dangerous corner of that stretch of road.

One can imagine what a view there was a hundred years ago from the mill situated on this winding country lane, diagonally opposite Poulton View Farm, which is still there. As far as the eye could see, to St Chad's parish church, lay meadows with such evocative names as Kate's Field, Weld's Meadow, Weld's Old Woman's Field, Great Snide, Little Snide and Swinley's Marsh, all bordered with hawthorn hedges. The occasional train stopped at Poulton Curve Halt, and heavy farm carts lumbered to Poulton village on market days, when cattle and geese were also herded along. Even in those days there was grumbling about the sharp bend and the narrowness of the track.

Other Fylde Mills

It's a pity that Dick's Mill is no longer in evidence, for the windmills of the Fylde, about forty in all, go back many centuries. There was even one built on the seashore at Rossall.

Both Thornton and Carleton Mills are mentioned in Domesday Book. Although Thornton became the larger and more important, Carleton's, like the others in the Fylde, would be a favourite place to meet friends and neighbours to catch up with the news.

For many years two millstones survived from Parkinson Tomlinson's cornmill, which was pulled down many years ago in Poulton-le-Fylde. For years they were under allotments, but with the help of Walter Heapy and the Thornton Windmill Preservation Society they were uncovered and put on show to interest the coachloads who rolled up, especially during the summer, to see the mill and hear about Edward Freeborn, one miller with a family of eight, who worked at grinding corn and filling sacks with golden grain in the 1890s.

Miller Edward Freeborn with his family, 1897.

The rest of the area's windmills are either gone entirely, completely transformed, or exist only as remains. Once a glebe mill, Clifton's was built by that famous eighteenth-century millwright Ralph Slater: a huge six-storey tower belonging to the powerful Clifton family. The ruined windmill on Carr Hill, Kirkham (one of the highest points of the Fylde which was once a Roman look-out post, first stop coastwards from the important camp of Preston), was one of a long line, for records show that

A millstone from Poulton Mill.

there was a glebe mill there 300 years ago. The ruin was converted into a super home, Wynde Milne, by Mr and Mrs James Dean over a period of eighteen months some years ago, but the photographs dated 1918 show a sorry-looking mill with broken stumps for sails. A legend tells of a red-haired ghost that haunted this mill and set things on fire with his hair - surely a folksy throw-back to the perennial bogey of fire.

A settlement from 29 September 1685 refers to Sir Thomas Clifton of Lytham granting the parsonage of Kirkham . . . one barn, one hay house, also a pasture called Close with a Carr, also two oxganges under the Windmill Hill and Dale Brigg also Nanni Flatt, also the windmill with other oxgang in the Common Town Field . . . also parcel in Kirkham of Marsh called Kirkholm'.

The old timber glebe mill at Kirkham ended its days in 1812 to be replaced by the brick one, which was leased to Christopher and John Waddington. What the Waddingtons could not have foreseen was that the owners of Carr Hill House would plant trees which eventually formed a windbreak, making their mill usable only under certain conditions. John Waddington complained that he had to pay more ground rent than the miller at Lytham but his pleas were unanswered, his business failed and he and his family were beggared.

Hambleton Mill met its demise in 1902 when the wooden post or

Marsh Mill (also known as Thornton Mill) and Thornton village,
nineteenth century. This mill was built by Bold Fleetwood Hesketh.

peg which turned the peg mill into the wind wore out and could not be replaced. After that the mill became ruinous. In its lifetime, however, it was a favourite subject for artists and a sketch dated 1850, made by a Trinity House inspector living in Fleetwood, is still in his family. Looking at this sketch book I could scarcely believe my eyes. There, alongside onion-domed buildings sketched in Russia, was one of 'our' peg mills.

Preesall Mill, built in 1839 to replace a post mill blown down in a gale, another of Ralph Slater's, was the scene of a wager. A farm worker, hoping for full and high circles, was tied to one of the 38ft long sails. Bets were laid and excitement ran high, but after one revolution the poor chap begged to be hauled down. This mill, worked by the Bisbrown family, was used by Trinity House, featuring as New Mill in Captain H.M. Denham's 1840 hydrographic survey. Plotted along coasts and estuaries, inns, farms, lighthouses and windmills served as guides to the mariner, and owners had to whitewash structures to throw them into stark relief.

Warton Pegmill lay ruined in 1915. A long pole terminating in a cartwheel used to turn the mill into the wind. A 6ft protective wall was

The old windmill at Pilling, 1959. Without its sails the highest windmill in the Fylde looks sadly gaunt.

built around it and the interior was reached by a primitive wide ladder from the ground. The mill stones were unusually large, 5ft 10in in diameter, but there was only one pair. Before 1717 this mill was on the other side of the Ribble. It was taken to pieces, packed up and ferried across to Guides House to be re-assembled at Warton. Similarly a Kirkham peg mill (1780) was taken down and transported across the Ribble to Birkdale, rather like the do-it-yourself packs of today. Iron horseshoes were nailed about Warton mill, but good luck deserted it when it was finally swept away to make room for an airfield.

From the crest of the old Roman track to the River Ribble it was once possible to see four working windmills: Weeton, Singleton, Marton, Staining. Indeed, fourteen were visible from the top of the tower of Poulton-le Fylde's parish church.

The last mentioned was situated in a lane, once part of the old Roman road or track from Freckleton Naze on the River Ribble to

Skippool on the River Wyre. Staining Mill was quite different from others in windmill land. It had no rear fantail, its top having to be turned into the wind to set the sails whirling. A big wheel, the size of a cart-wheel, was fixed outside the top storey and fitted with a long rope that reached to the ground, acting as a pulley, to achieve this burdensome job. Comparatively small as windmills go (or went), Staining's nineteenth-century mill strikes me as a 'do it yourself' job. It was the only mill in the Fylde operated this way. It also had sails on which canvas could be placed and taken off, like the sails on a ship, according to the mood of the wind, an idea almost medieval in its conception. Its dusty, floury interior was brightened by ballads and broadsheets pasted thickly over the brick walls. Ancient advertisements for patent medicines (Floriline 'cured' baldness) mingled with playbills announcing visits of the Barnstormers to Poulton Tithe Barn in their frequent performances of *Maria Marten or Murder in the Red Barn*. Even the weathervane was different. In the shape of a fish instead of a cock, this must have been considered more appropriate as Staining was so close to the Irish Sea. With moving parts salvaged from a primitive bicycle – and matching the creaking pulley wheel for quaintness – the flat metal fish veered to and fro on the topmost part of the mill four storeys up, utterly at the caprice of Fylde breezes but with the best view of the village. It was certainly a good site for a windmill, the remains of which went back 200 years. At the time of the Reformation, Lawrence Rigson was the miller, the rent for his house and windmill £2 annually.

Customs and Skills
The Dowager Duchess of Norfolk's will of 19 February 1745 left her mill and land at Carleton to relations, the Weld family, that name accounting for the old name of Castle Gardens (the Weld Inn, later Weld's Arms) and field names surrounding the inn. It makes reference to 'paying multure according to the custom and usage of this said Miln . . . the grinding of such corn and malt in her Grace's Manor of Carleton', and also to Her Grace's Court Baron which could enforce the duties of the tenantry in connection with the corn mill. Benevolent maybe, but villagers had to go to the lord of the manor's corn mill and pay him for the privilege of grinding their corn. Under this custom, called mill soke, he could prevent the building of a rival mill. Payment was placed in the multure bowl or toll dish, the miller taking his in kind, which gave rise to

Thornton Mill, 1870. A nineteenth-century custom was to set the sails in a cross when a funeral party was passing.

Chaucer and others believing that some millers cheated, but most were reckoned jolly, performing a vital task for the community. Not only were vigilance and strength called for, but experience was required in order to achieve fine and consistent grinding. This was determined by the speed of the millstones, which in turn depended on the speed of the sails. The rate of adding grain, the dressing of the stone faces and the gap between also counted. Until Thomas Mead invented an automatic means of adjustment in 1787 this last, called tentering, was done by hand. If the sails became 'tail-winded' millers had to take immediate action to prevent cap and sails being blown away or, worse still, fire breaking out as heat and sparks were generated by the spinning machinery. Purists among them favoured hand-made cog wheels of apple-tree wood for smoothest running, but this fear of fire led to another custom, Mill Wake, a clock-round vigil in busy seasons. One graphic description in the *Lancaster Gazette* reports the burning calamity of Cockerham Mill, which further set fire to two thatched cottages. Like a sea captain the corn miller learned to ride out the storm of hurricane winds which visited windmill land every October. He could turn the sails edgewise to the wind or choke the millstones with grain to slow down action but the aim was to grind consistently. John Baron achieved this with his peg mill (all wood, so at even greater risk from fire). 'I think it's the best mill hereabouts . . . saw the miller in his winter garb,' wrote headmaster Hornby Porter, describing his annual visit in his diary on 15 January 1844. Of ancient origin, the wooden peg mills turned on a massive post, virtually a tree trunk sunk into the ground. John thus rotated his well-balanced structure by a protruding tail pole fitted with a cart wheel into the eye of every favourable wind.

'Goodbye Jennie'

Many tales proliferated over the centuries. One concerned the murder of a Scottish pedlar, a popular character who travelled around the Fylde selling ribbons, elastic and cloth. Just a few days before Christmas, having paused for refreshment at the Green Man, he set off along the lonely highway, resolved to sleep on the miller of Staining's couch that night, as was his custom. Not far from the mill he was brutally murdered by two sailors for his money. Crawling to its white-washed walls and using a finger dipped in his own blood Archie Cameron left a stark message for his wife, 'Goodbye Jennie'. The story goes that Jennie had a vision of the quaint mill with its thrashing fish. She set off to tour all the windmills in the Fylde till she came to, and recognised, the one at Staining, and the miller was able to tell her how he had found the poor pedlar. The miller's wife forbade the message ever to be washed off, for that would bring bad luck to the whole community.

The Abana

On another pre-Christmas night in 1894, 22 December, bad luck struck Staining Mill again. Out at sea Adolph Danielson, master mariner, struggled in a perfect hurricane to save his 1,200-ton wooden barque, *Abana*. No sooner had his crew clewed up the foresail than it blew away. Mizzen, fore topgallant, mainsail, topsail and fore upper topsail followed. As the ship drifted helplessly, her anchor fouled and she struck ground on Shell Wharfe to be driven finally on shore at Norbreck. Blackpool lifeboat took off all sixteen hands at 8pm, following the alert from the innkeeper, Robert Hindle. The little fish on top of Staining Mill went wild and the sails and mill suffered considerable damage. Richard Blacow, blacksmith, Joseph Crompton, miller, John Dewhurst, farmer

Cleveleys Hotel, from where the landlord sent word that the Abana *had been stranded in a great gale, December 1894. The hotel and thatched cottages have now gone.*

from Staining Hall, and the rest of the population scattered around the hamlet had plenty to talk about the following day when newspaper headlines ran: 'Cyclone, 120mph strikes NW coast of Lancashire'. Wind instruments were broken and *Abana* was not alone in her struggles. The *Duke of York* steamer from Belfast, carrying 400 terrified passengers all looking to being home for Christmas, eventually made landfall at Fleetwood with top deck gear washed away. Captain John Cook and Chief Mate Mr Higham declared it the worst cyclone they had ever experienced. To this day the remains of the *Abana* can still be seen, according to the shifting of tides. The magnificent ship's bell now hangs in the north-west porch of St Andrew's Church, Cleveleys, to ring out at every service for the interment of ashes. As for Staining Mill's fish, canvas sails and wheel, they too 'sailed' into history.

Goodbye Windmill Land

What a wonderful sight it must have been in the sixteenth century, the moving sails of forty peg mills; even in the nineteenth there were more than twenty reaching from sea and rivers to busy Preston. Artists sketched and painted them. Charles Dickens, Keir Hardie, Mr Pitt the statesman, Cobden and Bright, Vesta Tilley, Caruso and Madame Patti were but a few to glimpse them or to visit. However, at the turn of the century demand was for fine flour. Some mills ground only for farm use; sails gradually ceased turning; pegs and caps rotted; trees grew out of and birds and rabbits nested in the ruins. Pictorially we lost much in their passing. Peeling, shrunken, sails gone, gone also was the dignity and character – but there are moves afoot for restoration. The smell of freshly ground corn floating over lanes laden with hawthorn blossom and the clack of mills must have been very satisfying. So thought I, purchasing a kilo of stone-ground, wholemeal flour from a recently restored windmill in Norfolk.

Lytham's windmill was first mentioned in the twelfth century; this building was constructed in 1802. It now has a museum in its basement and has had new sails fitted.

Chapter Seven
SCHOOLS

The founder of Carleton village school was Elizabeth Wilson of Whiteholme in Carleton, who made a will on 22 September 1680 desiring that a quarter of her goods be invested in land, the profit from which to be used by the Overseers of Carleton to educate the poor of the township. This was added to by Richard Singleton on 17 May 1697 when he conveyed a close of land called Carr Hey to be used for the same purpose. A sum of money left by William Bamber, yeoman of Carleton, in 1688 – '£40 to be for ever disposed of for the benefit of the poor inhabitants and the poor children . . . within Great Carleton Side' – was let out to gain interest. The money accruing from this was to go to poor inhabitants, 20*s* being reserved for the buying of books or paying school wages. William also left 1*s* 6*d* to each of his godchildren and 40*s* to the vicar, trusting the churchwardens of the whole parish that the sum was wisely used. Income from rents in 1717 amounted to £22 18*s* 0*d*, which was paid annually to the schoolmaster, who had between thirty and fifty children in his care. In these bequests and others that followed once again the lovely field names crop up, so telling of history: Great Field, The Croft, New Hay, Two Carrs, Great Meadows. The inhabitants built a school 'on waste land called Four Lane Ends' belonging to Sir Nicholas Sherburne who then held the manor, and who granted it for 500 years at a rent of 1*s* per annum.

The efforts of yeoman farmers in the Carleton area built another school on the site in 1839. In many of the photographs the cobble wall surrounding it can be seen, made from pebbles from the seashore. The school always had a reputation for producing good scholars. There was indeed a brilliant mathematician instructing at Carleton village school during the nineteenth century. Miss Livesey recalled the school that replaced this one and described it as 'first rate, with big windows, parquet floor, cloakrooms, gas, etc.' Time has marched on still further to replace that school also, and the present one stands in spacious grounds on a site a little further away from the corner, opposite Castle Gardens.

The tercentenary celebrations of Carleton C of E School, 1680–1980. Mr Wrightson, the headmaster, is on the right.

Baines Endowed School, founded in 1717 by James Baines, woollen merchant, has also concerned Carleton: the trust set up under the Baines Charities involved £800 for the purchase of lands, half of the profits to the use of the poor population of Poulton and the other half to apprentice children yearly in Marton, Hardhorn, Carleton and Thornton. One poor boy was apprenticed to Mr Scott 'to learn the mysteries of Punch and Judy'. Reports on and references to 'James Baines's Poor and

Class Four at Carleton School, 1984. The teacher is Mrs Siddall.
(Joan Hart)

Apprenticing Charity' crop up regularly in the minutes of Carleton parish meetings, which were held in Carleton schoolroom. On 31 December 1899, for example, the balance in hand was £43 8s 10d. Mr William Jemson, farmer at White Carr, wanted this to go towards the building of a new school in Carleton, but under the terms of James Baines's will this could not be done. The Commissioners also tried to have two scholarships to Baines School allotted to Carleton boys. It was alleged that two free scholarships had been available to Carleton township, but not having been used had been passed to Hardhorn. The meeting on 6 March 1899 reported that the Education Authorities had condemned the little cobble-walled school built in 1839.

A solitary 'dame school', privately run, existed in Carleton in the 1890s near Gibson's confectioner's shop, but it did not last long as there were three others on a grander scale in Poulton.

It is interesting to remember that in these early days, looking from Carleton village across to what had been Thornton Marsh, only fields, hedges, farm buildings, Thornton windmill, village, church and the Bay

Baines Endowed School.

Horse Inn would be seen. The Bay Horse was Lawrence Almond's Beer House where the trustees of Baines Charity School, Thornton, met annually. It was Candlemas when farmers paid their rent and from this the trustees paid the schoolmaster, Mr Thomas Parkinson, his salary, setting aside 10s for themselves for 'a sumptuous meal' at the inn.

Readings from the 1877 Education Act, which was issued to parents and employers, could usefully be applied today. Besides enforcing school attendance, if any child was habitually found wandering aimlessly, causing damage to property, etc., the result was a fine to the parents.

The Little Schools on the Moss
In these bleak days when teaching jobs, because of falling rolls and failing funds, are no longer sacrosanct, it is mildly therapeutic to searchlight the pedagogue's lot of a hundred years ago. Taking but one small sample from the Thornton with Fleetwood Board School Minutes, surprising comparisons emerge. What happened when the School Board, consisting of two parsons, a yeoman-farmer and two 'gentlemen' decided to build a school on the lonely marsh? Well, they moved fast and kept a tight hand on the purse strings. From the first meeting on 10 January

1878, at the Whitworth Institute, things took just two years to complete.

A census made by Mr Clegg, the poor rate collector, had revealed 232 children between three and sixteen in the area, but the plan approved for the New Board School attached was to accommodate ninety. Out of nine architects' submissions that of Mr J.A. Seward of Preston was accepted on 14 November 1878 and a deed of conveyance was quickly drawn up by Mr Ascroft, solicitor. Meanwhile two worthies from the School Board, Mr Tyler and Captain Martin, had procured a site from Mrs Warbreck between Thornton church and Fisher's Fold for £260. Land was then 5s a yard. Richard Jones, a builder who owned ships that sailed from the new docks at Fleetwood, offered to erect their school for £1,258. His tender was accepted because it was the lowest. When the water-supply pipe was laid, all 680ft of it, in September 1879, tenders ranging from £25 to £130 were considered – but T.A. Drummond was their man because his was inclusive of Fylde Water Works charges.

The little school at Carleton Moss, built in 1836 and photographed in 1879. The boundary wall is made of pebbles gathered from the seashore. (Chris Gleave)

The school on Carleton Moss, c. 1900.

When it came to selecting a capable master, terms firmly laid down that the successful candidate 'must be married and his wife competent to teach sewing'. Thirty-six applications from all over the country poured into this little Fylde backwater, from as far away as Barnsley, Manchester, Hereford, Huntingdon, Shrewsbury, and guess what the Board decided? They would pay no more than £80 per annum, which was what Mr J.H. Revill of West Bromwich requested. Rash applicants had quoted £110, even £120 per annum. Naturally they were turned down. So was Mr Revill in the end, because a certain Mr J.M. Carter of Nottingham agreed to do the job for £75! At about the same time a reminder was sent to the managers of Thornton Free School, one of three set up under the will of James Baines, woollen draper, in 1717, that their school must be brought up to the standard required by the Education Acts or they 'would have to build new'.

On 20 January 1880 a grand opening concert was held on the new premises, which were also to earn their living as night school. Gravelling the paths was sorted out by the new master from tenders submitted by local workmen. Again the lowest of the low was selected, paths being laid for the sum of £10. Mrs Cowell of Fisher's Fold was paid 1s 6d for cleaning the school.

After a gruelling year it was obvious even to the Board that eighty scholars were too many for one teacher so Annie Carter, the schoolmaster's wife, was roped in as assistant – a snip at £20 per year. In order to eke out their existence the Carters grew vegetables and fruit in the garden of the school house. They also kept a few hens but there is no mention of free coals, as was sometimes the case.

Any child 'wilfully' absent on a day of inspection, when the Rev. George Steel, HM Schools Inspector, turned up was fined 6*d*, but if he or she attended at the next inspection 3*d* of that was returned.

The Carters produced some good scholars, as did the little school on Carleton Marsh not far away.

Chapter Eight
AROUND AND ABOUT

Hambleton

Villages close to Carleton were often like Hambleton, scattered over a 3 to 4 mile radius. By 1864 Hambleton had Shard Bridge, built over the Wyre at a cost of £13,000. Built wholly of iron and 325yds long, it has now been dismantled, but for over 100 years it was able to do away with the ferry boats which once conveyed people to Poulton and Singleton.

This hag stone was found at Hambleton when a traditional cruck-built cottage was demolished in 1997. These were placed on farms to scare off witches.

Hambleton, 1902.

Singleton

The 'model villages' of Great Singleton and Little Singleton, about 2 miles from Carleton, were described in Barretts Directory as 'a township and ecclesiastic parish comprising 2,874 acres of fertile, well-cultivated land with a parish council of five. T.H. Miller, Charles E.D. Atkinson and Thomas Catlow being the owners of the soil. In 1841 the population was 391. A low thatched chapel built by Joseph Hornby was replaced with St Anne's Church with a tower and six bells. It was Squire T.H. Miller that provided it along with model cottages and a school in 1863.'

Stalmine and Stainhall

These two villages constituted a township and chapelry in the parliamentary division of Lancaster with six names on the parish council. The manor of Stalmine formerly belonged to the monks of Furness, but at the dissolution of the monasteries became Crown property. St James's Church was rebuilt in 1806 on the old site, which dates back to 1246.

One of the most interesting buildings in the remote village of Stalmine was the old Grange, which adjoined the churchyard. Some say there was a secret passage from the Grange to the church.

The gates at the entrance to the grounds of Singleton Hall, Squire Miller's mansion. Carleton and Singleton Morris dancers performed together here on gala days.

The post office and Seven Stars Inn, Stalmine, c. 1901.

Plans of Stalmine Hall Estate with its valuable farms reveal what was offered for auction in July 1890: excellent wine and beer cellars, two larders, spacious entrance hall, dining room, drawing room, breakfast room, library, kitchen, butler's pantry and so on, as well as 'well-walled kitchen gardens and orchards'.

Wardleys

An ancient port in the township, Wardleys once served Poulton: vessels of 300 tons burden called here, their cargoes ranging from oranges to slaves. Population stood at 508 in 1851. Public subscriptions provided a town's reading room at Town Foot.

In 1940 the Wyre froze – as did marl pits, ponds, lakes and even the sea. This is Wardleys old port.

Hardhorn-with-Newton

This also included the hamlet of Staining. They were in the Fylde Union, with five members. In 1841 the population was 358. Baines Endowed Grammar School (one of three schools provided by James Baines, woollen merchant, who died in 1717) was restored in 1881. There are

Staining School, Class 4 boys, c. 1902. Fourth from left (front) is Robert Hawthornthwaite, son of Thomas, the miller at Marsh Mill. Scholars from here and from Carleton School saw their first aeroplane flying from Staining Hill near the windmill in the early 1900s.

Staining Mill, c. 1900.

sixty-two farmers listed. One of the Carleton Penswicks then ran Puddle House Farm, long notorious for a race of super rats. James Baines's farm at Staining, which provided towards the upkeep of the schools he founded, was in 1924 cultivated by Thomas Haythornthwaite, who was related to the corn miller of Thornton.

School, smithy, windmill and a cluster of thatched cottages strung along the hawthorn-hedged lanes made up Staining. Staining Hall, once very important, had become a farm but still retained traces of its moat from the days when the powerful Abbots of Whalley and the wealthy Singleton family dined there.

A pedlar calls, with his pack of pins, needles, elastic, ribbon and combs. He was a welcome visitor in the nineteenth and early twentieth centuries, especially in remote villages that had no shops. (Mr R. Irving)

Warton

This village is close to Kirkham. It had six members on its parish council, its population in 1841 being 552. Here were listed forty-three farmers. The once powerful Clifton family owned most of the land. John Margerison farmed at Boggart House, which according to local gossip had a resident boggart or elf of a mischievous turn of mind. Even in the early 1920s there were many country people who still believed that 'will o' the wisp', the flickering marsh gas from Carleton, Winmarleigh, Thornton and Pilling Mosses, was a spirit to beware of. Carleton moss or marsh was one of the largest of its kind.

Bispham

A very near neighbour of Carleton, a stroll across the fields if you wished to avoid the old, winding drovers' road. It was an important neighbour too, for here is Bispham parish church, the mother church. From 1190 to 1820 it was the only church in the whole of Bispham and Blackpool , so all weddings and funerals took place here. The baptismal registers date back to 1599. Marriage registers and burial registers go back to 1632. From the first church can still be seen the Norman arch of red sandstone. That goes back to the days of William Rufus, son of the Conqueror. In 1773 a gallery for the musicians was built, reached from steps outside the church. Instead of an organ they played a violin, cello, bassoon and

Bispham, c. 1890.

Another early photograph of Bispham.

Bispham parish church, 1939.

On the left of this photograph is Bispham Smithy, c. 1960.

ARP (Air Raid Precautions) training on Bispham Cliffs in 1938, the year before war was declared.

clarinet. The churchyard is also full of history, with its pilgrim's cross and burials going back to the days of sail. They include victims of the *Ocean Monarch* (1848) and the captain and crew of the *Favourite*, who were drowned off Bispham on 24 August 1848.

Thornton-Cleveleys

Victoria Road, now the main road of Thornton-Cleveleys, was originally Ramper Road, the name derived from Ramparts or banks enclosing the marshland. Bold Fleetwood Hesketh, uncle of Sir Peter Hesketh Fleetwood, was responsible for these.

The unruly sea used to flood over the fields as far inland as Thornton Church. Thomas Parr of Parr's Cottage grumbled bitterly and got his rates reduced, but Parr's Lane had its name changed to Meadows Avenue to commemorate a vicar of Thornton parish church, Mr Meadows, who presided around the time of Queen Victoria's Jubilee.

It was the coming of the railway that transformed the villages of Thornton and Cleveleys.

The village of Thornton, 1906, when it was truly rural.

Thornton Urban District Council's steam roller, c. 1928.

Thornton Urban District Council's fire engine, 1937.

Old cottages in Cleveleys, from a postcard sent in 1912.

The opening of Jubilee Gardens on Thornton-Cleveleys Promenade to mark the Silver Jubilee of George V and Queen Mary, 1937.

Lord Stanley unveils the Jubilee Gardens monument, 1937.

Along the Coast

There were of course lots of easy walks through the fields from Carleton and even children were known to walk many miles. Fresh winds blowing from the Irish Sea brought thoughts of picnics and paddling. Cleveleys coast had a wild, unspoilt look with seapinks, sea lavender, burnet rose, sea holly, rocket and marram grass growing among sandhills. There was an abundance of different kinds of sea shells, all of which the Rev. Mr Thornber listed in 1837.

Before sea defences were built, dwellings near the sea, like Fanny Hall and Carr Houses, were washed away by coast erosion. One man in 1730 'left as much space when bounding his bank as would allow four roads, supposing that sufficient, but his four roads were washed away'.

Supreme on this stretch of sea coast there once stood Cleveleys Hydro with its hydropathic baths, tennis courts, resident orchestra and eighteen-hole golf course. Tennis teas, palm court orchestra, shady hats and straw 'cadies' are things of the past. This large area is now packed with houses.

The Rev. William Thornber, who wrote a local history of Blackpool and the surrounding area in 1837.

The Railway – and Tourism Begins

The glorious days of steam travel have also slipped into the history books. The Preston and Wyre Railway with its terminus at Fleetwood was intended to transform and develop the Fylde. The line opened in 1840 but Ramper, the first station to serve the Thornton-Cleveleys area, was closed as early as 1843 because it was financially unsuccessful. A station called Cleveleys was opened in 1865 close to the old Ramper but the name was changed again to Thornton-for-Cleveleys on 1 April 1905. Eventually (it really was a case of *plus ça change*) in the mid-1920s a signboard went up: 'Thornton-Cleveleys'. Holiday crowds five deep lined the length of Thornton station as the popularity of Cleveleys rocketed: 85,693 passengers in 1913; 138,164 in 1924. Sixty-two trains made stops daily in summer but passenger services were withdrawn altogether on 1 June 1970. Perhaps the last great expression was made when *Oliver Cromwell* thundered to a halt there on the occasion of a special trip for 'gricers' (as railway enthusiasts are known).

Building the Preston and Wyre Railway, 1838: a lithograph by William Gawin Herdman of Liverpool.

The nearest Carleton got to the railway was a request stop at Poulton Curve, until a serious accident on this dangerous bend in 1893 stopped the practice.

Chapter Nine
BLACKPOOL

Try Blackpool, England

arleton, although it remained Sleepy Hollow, had within walking distance the glitter of Blackpool. Three words summed up the fame of its close neighbour when a postcard from Israel, in the nineteenth century, addressed simply 'The North Pier' was endorsed 'Try Blackpool, England' by the postal authorities – and it arrived!

America's Coney Island, the famous amusement beach, was the only rival to be taken seriously, but for sheer continuous, innovative, spectacular entertainment presented in gutsy, rip-roaring style, Blackpool still emerges supreme. Add to the mixture a grand capacity to explore the freakish, bizarre and unexpected, to shock, to tickle appetite, to startle, yet to delight and you almost have the essence. Living up to a world-beating tradition of boldness and brashness brooks neither the timorous nor the tardy approach, and bright, breezy, bracing Blackpool could never be so accused.

Backed by that majestic landmark, Blackpool Tower, a 519ft tapering intricacy of metal girders, to visitors in their millions North Pier is Blackpool, the interests of Pier and Tower being so blended that one without the other is unthinkable. 'Progress', the obvious motto from early municipality days, was the watchword, but even from its embryo state, when Blackpool was a fishing village by a very black pool which flowed into the sea from Marton's Moss, going one better seemed to be in the genes.

Modelled on Paris's Eiffel Tower, Blackpool Tower is a great success story. Seven thousand people a day travel skywards, and guess what they look for first? The North Pier. When the first pile was screwed into the clay on 27 June 1862, Major Francis Preston, Chairman of the North Pier Company, prophesied that it would grow into 'one of the most amazing aggregations of public amusement in the world'. On 21 May 1863, this 1,405ft long structure into which had gone 12,000 tons of metal was opened. For this red-letter holiday the townspeople insisted on bringing back the town crier, relegated by 'progress' as an anachronism, out of step with the march of time. His stentorian roars couched in record-breaking decibels greeted trippers spilling out of the Lancashire and Yorkshire trains which had been chuffing in from all directions since dawn. Fun-loving spirit overflowed; so did the pubs. Flags and bunting galore fluttered in the salty air while daredevils threatened to dive off the end of the pier. Some did.

Incidentally, aquatics became a speciality of the North Pier, its water deciding some of the principal championship events in the swimming world. Major Preston's twelve-pounder cannon, the only piece of artillery Blackpool could boast, vied with the town crier.

Supported by several brass bands, a grand procession of freemasons, friendly societies, fishermen, bathing machine attendants, lifeboatmen, dignitaries and the multitude proclaimed to the country 'this substantial and safe means for visitors to walk over the sea'. None other than the engineers of Brighton Pier would do. The gala opening was considered worthy of a front-page engraving in the *Illustrated London News*. Within three years they added a jetty for pleasure steamers *Queen of the Bay* and *Clifton*, but the restless, ambitious directors craved even more limelight, using fabulous personalities to promote their ways. They increased the area by another 5,000sq. yds to give the Pier its greatest glory, an Indian pavilion on the north wing. Totally authentic, this was designed from studies of Hindu palaces and temples, principally the Temple of Binderabad. Results were sufficiently spellbinding to hit news headlines in such tributes as 'strongest and most beautiful pier in Europe'. He who dares wins, mused the directors, headed by H.C. McCrea; when the prophets of doom were brushed aside for declaring it was tempting providence to build anything in the way of the tide, the Blackpool Pier Company had only had £12,000 in the kitty. Certainly this spirit of enterprise made North Pier without rival in the country.

That distinguished beauty Princess Louise, Duchess of Argyll, drew more crowds when she opened the widened Promenade in 1912. North Pier's entrance was set back, harmonising with and enlarging the square where people congregated. An arcade of shops in an onion-domed pavilion made for further enhancement without danger of sea-sickness.

Catastrophes too pulled the crowds. A large Norwegian barque, *Sirene*, helpless in the grip of a storm, smashed against the south side of the entrance in 1892, sweeping away six shops; the crew scrambled up girders onto the pier planking, one occasion when there was no need for the lifeboat to put to sea! Next day, for news travelled fast, crowds scrabbled for sodden furs and costume jewellery strewn on the sands by the next tide. Even more spectacular was the foundering of the *Foudroyant*, Lord Nelson's flagship, in June 1897. This wooden sailing

Foudroyant, *Lord Nelson's flagship, was wrecked off Blackpool in 1897.*

A rough sea at Blackpool, viewed from Central Pier, 1905.

ship was anchored for exhibition purposes. The captain, unaware of what the Irish Sea could wreak with its sudden summer storms, was astonished to find his ship wrecked off the North Pier, pounded by waves 60ft high. Drifting heavy oak timbers did hefty damage and again the crowds poured in (my father among them) to collect souvenirs. All sorts of objects were made from the oak and copper of this incomparable vessel and sold like hot cakes.

For a town constantly on the up, all this marked the advent of a new era of enterprise, a town whose only problem was accommodating its population explosion. But where there was a will there was a way. Six in a bed and working shift systems, or sharing horses' hay, who cared as long as they had arrived in Blackpool?

Pleasing everyone in this stately pleasure-dome (all human life is there from toddlers to granddads) is epitomised in the 'wish you were here' postcards: hard-working landladies with hearts of gold and HP sauce on groaning tables, large-bosomed nagging wives, henpecked husbands, bucket and spade Mabel Lucie Attwell children, and red-nosed boozers are all fair game for vulgar depiction, but somehow they emerge as hearty and healthy as the tangy sea breezes trying to whip them off the stands.

Amazingly, alongside this crude, rude health, in the golden years before fire destroyed the Indian Pavilion, some of the greatest instrumental and vocal artists in the world performed before Blackpool audiences: Sir Charles and Lady Hallé, Sims Reeves, Madame Patti, Signor Foli, Mr D. Ffrangson Davies and countless other celebrities, now a study in nostalgia. The North Pier's reputation for high-class orchestral music was established by Edward de Jong, possibly the most eminent flautist of his day. Masterly batons brought the North Pier concerts to the favourable notice of the best critics who spread the glad news through the national press. Professor Simon Speelman, linked with Manchester's Hallé Orchestra as an eminent viola player, further increased its fame.

Blackpool's Great Wheel, 1923.

My father, still making his annual pilgrimage to Blackpool in the 1950s, gloried in the music of Toni and the North Pier Orchestra. He sat ensconced for fleeting hours like a lord 'spreading his fat', as he put it, in the sun lounge with a brown paper bag of Victoria plums on his lap. In the same spot Raymond Wallbank played the organ (50 pence a deckchair to bask in tropical warmth). Today can be found Little Italy – half-price Capo di Monte ornaments, Bernard Delfont's Showtime with David Copperfield and Lenny Henry (Danny La Rue performed up the road), the Copper Cove, North Pier Joke Box, Miss Blackpool Bathing Competition, Madame Lovell, Palmist and Clairvoyant, and the Merrie England Bar. Serried banks of deckchairs face the sun at 30 pence a session for turning brick-red or Benidorm brown as the spirit moves you; or to cool off there are deep-sea fishing competitions from the jetty, gate money a mere 10 pence. The pier itself is free.

This summer season, to the rumbustious hundreds of thousands thronging the Golden Mile, clutching candy floss and 'Kiss Me' hats in breezes guaranteed to knock any self-respecting cobweb for six, big-eyeing Coral Island but making for the North Pier, all this represents value for money: a looking forward to autumn and the Blackpool Illuminations, the 'greatest free show on earth', 5 miles of illuminated tableaux and fairy lights – naturally. Where else?

Year after year unassailable Blackpool sets itself up for the race it has never stopped running.

All round our coast there are piers in parlous states, but not so North Pier, England. Stronger than when it was originally built, it remains Blackpool's trump card.

Bob Bickerstaffe

'Blackpool Tower is a landmark in the moral as well as the physical sense as it stands as an assurance that one day the earth may be inherited, if not by the meek, at least by clear consciences and stout hearts.'

These are the words of my great friend Harry Hodgkinson, a world-wide traveller who worked tirelessly for the welfare of Albania and was honoured with a decoration and a state funeral. Sooner or later Harry always returned to his roots. He was a great admirer of Blackpool's enterprise, especially the part played by the Bickerstaffe family. 'If John Bickerstaffe had been in charge of the building of the Tower of Babel,' joked Harry, 'it would have been halfway to the moon and we would all be speaking Sanskrit.'

Yachting and bathing at Blackpool, 1917.

Generations back the Bickerstaffes hailed from the hamlet of that name near Ormskirk. A family of fishermen, they lived in one of three cottages close to Foxhall, the Tyldesleys' historic residence, opposite Central Pier. Tourists, who walked south beyond the 200yds of grassed promenade, bought refreshments from one of the cottages, which prompted the Bickerstaffes to operate pleasure boats.

When Squire Talbot Clifton decided to sell off his holdings in the late 1840s, Edward Bickerstaffe, the head of the family, decided to buy the old manorial village pound opposite their cottage, which originally had been used for rounding up stray sheep and cattle, and build a boatyard on the site. Edward took his nephew Young Bob with him, who, incidentally, was still called Young Bob when he was eighty. Asked by Clifton's agent, James Fair, how much they could offer, Young Bob stoutly replied, '£84'.

'Then,' said Fair, 'it looks as though you have a bargain.'

The Blackburn brewer, Matthew Brown, realised that the Bickerstaffes had not only got a great bargain but also a super site. 'Ted, why dooen't tha oppen a pub an' a few rooms for lodgers, like?' So the Bickerstaffes built not a boatyard but the Wellington Inn on the site of the manorial pound.

When the South Pier Jetty Company was formed it looked for a site near the centre of Blackpool, far enough from its rival the North Pier. The enterprising Bickerstaffes not only offered part of their land as a forecourt entrance free of charge, but also acted as bankers, lending cash from the proceeds at the Wellington in order to pay the wages at the pier. At that time the only bank operating in Blackpool was the Preston Bank, for just one day a week, and even this was temporarily suspended in the 1860s when it ran into trouble. The Bickerstaffe loan represented a commitment to a potentially valuable commercial enterprise.

South Jetty, or Central Pier as it now is, did not turn out to be a good investment. By 1870 it had no manager, so Young Bob was persuaded to take on the job for at least one season. Legend has it that, looking across to crowded North Pier after counting only thirteen people on his own pier, he plastered the town with bills advertising cheap steamer outings and hired a German band to play for dancing when the overloaded boat got back. Bob had found his vocation!

Steamers ran to Barrow, Douglas, Liverpool and Llandudno. Not surprisingly, one of the favourites bore the name *Bickerstaffe*. Even more important, the rapidly increasing number of working-class visitors had discovered an entrepreneur who could meet their needs without condescension or censure. It never occurred to Bob, as it did to the North Pier Board, that 'there was to be no impropriety in the coming singing by the pier head concert party'. The crowds loved him, calling him Bob Snow because the front wall of his cottage was covered with bleached oyster shells. The man who, with grit, immense reserves of physical strength, an open mind and an outlay of £84 had won through, also earned admiration and respect for his service to others. He saved many lives at sea during his twenty-three years' sterling service when he skippered the lifeboat *Samuel Fletcher*. He designed a fishing boat and, with his extensive knowledge of the tides, was to give expert technical advice on the construction of sea defences. Thus the Bickerstaffes began to mould themselves into the most significant of the town's dynasties.

The erection of Gustave Eiffel's Tower for the Paris Exhibition of 1889 aroused great interest. Why should Blackpool not throw piers up into the sky as an earlier generation had thrown them out to sea? Opponents claimed that 7,000 tons of iron would surely collapse, but it went ahead. A City of London syndicate, Standard Contract and Debenture Corporation, bought Dr Cocker's aquarium site and building for £60,000 and sold it to the Blackpool Tower Company for £95,000. When shares were offered for sale to the public in July 1891 the financial press prophesied that the company would lose money and that the ironwork would have to be sold for scrap. Many people said that they had got on very well without a tower and 'there was no particular requirement for it now'. Local enthusiasm was so lukewarm that out of the year's Census figure of 23,845, 23,823 declined to subscribe, and the average holding was £150. The syndicate was left with 150,000 of the £1 shares.

The foundation stone was laid in September 1891 by the local MP, who left a record of his voice under it on one of Edison's recently invented cylinders. Two months later the company had to ask its shareholders for cash to pay the contractors. By now the market share price had fallen by half. The syndicate also had to agree to knock £20,000 off the price of the site, thus freeing the Tower Company from London influence.

Visitors to the Fylde in Edwardian days.

By this time John Bickerstaffe, a recent mayor and company director, had come to incarnate the spirit of Blackpool enterprise and was persuaded to associate himself with the project. Deciding on a show of strength and confidence in himself, he sold shares in other companies to buy up the tower shares dumped on the market by disillusioned investors. From an initial holding of 500 shares he ended up with 20,000, and persuaded local people with money to follow suit. When he, 'a Bickerstaffe who could tell a guinea from a goshawk', began to buy more shares in what appeared to be a dud company, it was time for folks to think again. Cash inflow kept just ahead of outgoings and all went merry as a marriage bell. History was repeating itself as when an earlier Bickerstaffe prevented Central Pier from collapse.

Having finally reached port under the helmsmanship of John Bickerstaffe, Blackpool Tower began its profitable career. The crew of grateful shareholders presented their captain with a 4ft silver model of the Tower. In 1912 John also received a massive silver salver and was made Freeman of the Borough, but his crowning glory was when he was knighted Sir John.

Innovation was his watchword and Whit Monday was just the day for it – every year. He saw the first cinema show in the Tower Ballroom, when for a few magic moments the steamboat *Queen of the North* flickered across the silver screen.

Let Harry, who knew him well, have the last word. 'John Bickerstaffe looked rather like George V, only more alert and windswept. His beard was as white as the spume on a high spring tide. His eyes seemed half closed as though spanning not the promenade crowds but some dangerous and exotic horizon – the eyes of some high court judge deciding what sentence to give you.'

Chapter Ten
ENTERTAINMENT

Games

alking to old residents, in most cases they stress that although they lived well off the land there was no money to spare. In the 1930s pocket money was a penny a week. They read a great deal and played card games in the winter. In summer in the school yard or at 'the Top' – Four Lane Ends when there was no traffic – children played diabolo, bobs and checks, shuttlecock and battledore, hopscotch, skipping, whip and top, marbles ('murps'), hide and seek, 'nuts i' May'. Indoor games at Christmas time might be snapdragon, bobbing for apples, forfeits, blind man's buff, hunting the slipper, spinning the trencher, fortune telling or London Bridge. Older games which were dying out in the nineteenth century were 'cymbling for larks' and knur and spell, the latter no children's game but played for money, about £10 a side. One game played in a field near Raikes Hall in 1868 was reported: 'the play being twenty rise between Messrs W. Wilkinson and R. Rimmer, Manchester gentlemen visiting Blackpool. Rimmer after some good play made 120, his opponent 100. Mr W.E. Harrison of Southport acted as umpire.'

Customs

Some of the very old customs in Carleton and the Fylde go back further than any residents can recall, but today's world is showing much interest in reviving them. Ancient Morris and maypole dancing were still enjoyed with gusto when Miss Kate and Miss Alice Jane Livesey were young, the latter being born in the last century. The maypole in Carleton was set up at Pye's Farm. It was brought out once a year and carefully stored away after the ceremony. The children were well drilled in the routine. 'You had to be well ordered or you got in a terrible mess when it was being unravelled.' Miss Livesey's brother Billy started in the team of Morris dancers and eventually spent much time training new entrants. An eighteenth-century Fylde jingle of the Morris dancers was, 'We are come over the mire and moss. We dance an hobby horse. A dragon you shall see.'

Before Carleton Marsh was reclaimed one regular custom was 'beating the bounds' or 'riding the marsh'. Customarily performed on Ascension Day, all inhabitants with the leaders of the community walked the boundaries of the township. This must be of very old origin as the idea was to perpetuate and impress a memory of the boundary, especially on young persons. Small 'tags' or gratuities were offered to the boys who accompanied the group, in order to encourage their presence. On the outset each was presented with a willow wand. A 1682 reference to the custom, obviously well observed to protect land rights and boundaries, speaks of £1 being paid out of parish funds 'For fruit on Perambulation Day'. In the eighteenth century rushbearing was also observed when the rush cart assembled in Poulton before James Baines's house (which afterwards became the Custom House). The cart was dragged to the church where fresh rushes were strewn on the floor. Vestry book entries show that Thomas Parkinson was paid 6s 8d 'for rushes' and it was made into a merrymaking time with music and Morris dancing. On the occasion in 1765 the churchwardens spent 1s 6d. 'Ringing the pan', which Thomas Hardy refers to, was when a band of young men armed with pokers, fire-irons, pans, tongs and shovels, headed by the bellman, would assemble beneath a window and make a terrible racket. The unfortunate couple chosen were suspected of 'courting' on a Friday night, which old country people considered sinful.

Cock-fighting on Shrove Tuesday was popular all over the Fylde. Of bear baiting and bull baiting there is no evidence in Carleton, but a man with a shuffling dancing bear passed through. My mother, as a small child, remembered backing up against the bear and being terrified when she saw what it was, although even to her young senses the creature was pathetic and smelly.

Cole-seeding and the shutting of marling ceremonies were important in rural communities. Cole-seeding was when the whole neighbourhood helped each other; collecting, thrashing, winnowing the crop in the fields and 'housing' seed for market. All was done in an atmosphere of good humour, and after the toil came a big supper with dancing on the clay floor of the barn to the tune of the fiddle. Mr Haythornthwaite from Fleetwood was a favourite player on these occasions because he would go on all night. At harvest home a lord and lady were drawn out of the marl pit by strong horses decorated with ribbons and mounted by drivers who were also decked out and trimmed with sashes and coloured streamers. A glance at the map shows old Carleton covered with marl pits.

Annie Johnson, aged thirteen, the first Rose Queen in Lytham, 1894. Club Day processions had been held since 1881, but in 1894 the crowning of a Rose Queen by one of the Clifton family of Lytham Hall was inaugurated.

At Christmas came midnight carols and mince pies, which represented the offerings of the wise men. The mince pies were made from a spiced mixture within an old English coffin-shaped case to represent the infant Jesus's manger. Before dawn the young ones would be on the street calling, 'Get up old wives and bake your pies. 'Tis Christmas Day in the morning. The bells shall ring; the birds shall sing.' A breakfast of black puddings commenced the day, as usually a pig had been killed.

At Easter the village lads of Carleton, as a change from tying villagers' door handles together (a strange Christmas custom elsewhere in the countryside), performed a dance known as 'ignagning', later known as pace-egging. My father remembered this, but could not join in as he was lame. Nowadays it takes the more innocent form of rolling hard-boiled coloured eggs down a slope.

'Where the high stool hangs over the muddy pool' was where ducking bad-tempered women took place, and a cuckstool or 'tumbrel' was used in Carleton from Saxon times. The last reference to its actual use seems to be in 1837, when 'a woman called Idle was the last person to suffer'. The crowd had also 'ridden the stang' and sung the appropriate song at her door, which indicates that they were not satisfied with her morals either.

The first Monday after Twelfth Night was known as Plough Monday and was regarded as a general holiday. The ploughmen roamed from house to house asking for money, which they spent on ale. The plough was dragged along by sword dancers in procession, one labourer dressed as an old woman and another clad in skins with a tail hanging down his back. These two begged offerings from the waiting crowd, and if any householder refused to give money the plough was turned around to disturb the ground in front of his dwelling. The plough was known either as White Plough (referring to the mummers being dressed in white, gaudily trimmed with ribbons) or Fond or Fool Plough (meaning the whole ceremony was just a bit of fun).

Many special occasions had special foods associated with them. My great-great-grandfather Edward Hoghton made Braggat Ale at the Dog Inn, Belthorn, for Mothering Sunday. His parents haled originally from Yate and Pickup Bank, a tiny hamlet near Haslingden, where no doubt this ale was drunk on other occasions as well. Although no precise recipe is available, I know he added honey and ginger to the mulled ale. My father, born in Belthorn, later of Blackburn, always referred to Mothering Sunday as Fig Pie Sunday. Here is Mother's fig pie recipe. Make a good shortcrust pastry with 8oz lard and 16oz flour. Rub well in till the mixture resembles breadcrumbs. Made with lard the pastry can be rolled out thinly, which is the prerequisite of a good fig pie. Soak the dried figs in hot water and sugar, and cut into long strips to fill the pie dish generously.

I remember this as a gorgeous fruity pie to be indulged in before redcurrants, damsons, bilberries and raspberries became available again.

May Day Celebrations

In the days of old, ties and links between families often ceased during winter as roads were often impassable, under mud or snow. Candles made of rushes dipped in sheep's fat were the only means of light in cottages and there were few newspapers and interests outside the circle of the village, so the coming of spring had great significance. Not only was it a welcome change in a year of toil but also a renewal of friendship that had to cease during winter.

Friends and relatives flocked into the village on May Day for merry-making. Young folk on the village green danced the day away. While the old May Day revels were a survival held by the Romans in honour of Flora, the goddess of spring, Lancashire for fourteen centuries afterwards celebrated Bringing in the May – boughs of hawthorn covered with blossom as a sign that summer was coming. Great and Little Carleton had hedges laden with that sweet-smelling may blossom. Along with other Fylde villages the procession passed through Great Carleton, strewing flowers. Mummers sang and danced and the housewives came out to give them home-brewed wines and sweetmeats (later Wakes cakes).

A May Queen procession, Poulton, 1912. The little girls in front are Edith and Kathleen Danton. Two little chimney sweeps are in charge of the banner. The custom of blackened faces goes back centuries in the May Day revels. (Susan Donaldson)

In anticipation of May Day and its traditional festivities we may be sure that amid such events as the 'shutting of marl' when a 'lord and lady', bedizened, were dragged out of the marl pit by strong horses, equally tricked up, Jack-in-the-Green would be sure to make his presence felt. The walking hedge or Jack-in-the-Green was a long-established version of the Green Man who, in one guise or another, had long haunted Merrie England. In such a rural community as Carleton he would surely figure as we saw recently portrayed in the charming television production of *Cranford*. Witness also the number of ancient inns named the Green Man.

Even the chimney sweepers in London's Piccadilly featured this essence of spring in their May Day antics. 'Here they come! Here is the garland and their lord and lady. Their garland is a large cone of holly and ivy framed upon hoops. Within it is a man, wholly unseen and hence the garland has the semblance of a moving hillock of evergreens. . . .' (William Hine, 1825.)

On May Day there were also races and wrestling bouts for young men, and dances round the maypole until dark.

Saints' Days

It was a hard life but those who survived were hardy and long-lived. Agricultural labourers, of whom there were many in Carleton, had to wash under the pump on many an icy cold morning, so it was small wonder they snatched at any opportunity for fun. Favourite saints' days, once solemn wakes, gradually took on a lighter meaning, and the mingling of Celtic pagan practice with Christian ritual is well illustrated in Lammas tide, the ancient holiday which eventually became August bank holiday. 'Lamb Mass' was the time when tithe lambs were taken to the tithe barns and presented, rather unwillingly, to the church. Some think it denoted the feast when bread for the Holy Sacrament was made from the first corn of that year's harvest.

St James's Day on 25 July was popular as it heralded midsummer, approaching harvest and the traditional time of country fairs. A pilgrimage to St James's tomb at Compostella in Spain was an alternative to the longer and more dangerous pilgrimage to the Holy Land. The early 'wakers' each came back with a scallop shell, this being the saint's emblem. Several old grottoes by the sea on the south coast and on the Isle of Wight were built entirely of shells to commemorate the St James's Day fairs.

Soul cakes, made from oatmeal and aromatic seeds, were eaten on All Souls Day. Goosnargh still specialises in them. The innkeeper's wife at the Bushell's Arms used a grater a yard long for her cone of sugar in the 1900s. The eating of soul cakes, especially in Crookdale Lane, which led to the great Moss of Stalmine and Rawcliffe, signified that for every cake eaten one soul was freed from Purgatory, a prayer being said as you ate. Soul Mass became Saumas, another kind of spiced and sweetened cake. One Lancashire woman preserved a soul mass cake that had been in her family for a century: it was believed to bring good luck.

On the weekend after 12 August in the Fylde village of Stalmine, people ate tosset cakes on Tosset Sunday. St Oswald's was the old name for St James's Church, Stalmine – and Tosset was Oswald's nickname.

On the feast of St Giles dancing booths were set up and fiddlers were brought in. One villager boasted that he had 'danced his shoes right off his feet'.

Carleton Townswomen's Guild took part in Poulton Victorian Fair in 2000. A whole weekend was given up to stalls and exhibitions depicting Queen Victoria's reign.

Castle Gardens

A popular place of entertainment was the Castle Gardens Inn, which existed in the eighteenth century when it was referred to as 'Jenny Houlding's'. She was then proprietor and may have had something to do in name with Jenny's Fields (339 and 352 in the Tithe Schedules, bisected by Blackpool Road). In the 1841 census Elizabeth Smith presided, and the building was known as Weld's Arms, taking its name from local landowner J. Weld. In 1848 George Ibbotson was genial host, still calling time in 1851, although the directory had changed the spelling of his name to Ibison. William Roskell from the Fleetwood seafaring family was managing in 1865 and by 1871 the inn was referred to as Halfway House. It would most certainly be listed in timetables for wagonette trips, the publican in those days being Frederick Moore. It was still called Weld's Arms in the 1879 Slator's Directory, but in the 1890s Castle Hotel takes over as its title and the 1892 Barrett's Directory of the Fylde lists Arthur Fitzroy Thompson as victualler at the Castle Hotel – 'pleasure grounds and accommodation for visitors'. These were the days of many visitors. The railways had made trips to the seaside easy, and excursions into the picturesque countryside were possible in high wagonettes, accommodating twenty people at a time. In order to compete, Captain Thompson had created tea rooms, swing boats and well-laid-out gardens adjacent to the hotel. A description of it in 1896 was as follows: 'Castle Gardens, Carleton, the most popular hotel in the Fylde District. J.J. Tattersall, late of the Cross Keys Hotel, Blackfriars Road, London, has taken over the above noted hotel where he will be glad to welcome old and new friends. The neatest laid out gardens in the district. The Bowling Green has recently undergone considerable improvement and is now in the best of condition. Wines and spirits of the best quality. Strawberry and cream teas.'

In fierce competition were the Strawberry Gardens Hotel at Fleetwood, which grew masses of strawberries, had even larger grounds that could be entered from the shore, and also the Eagle and Child fruit and flower gardens at Weeton. Ralph Clough, proprietor at Weeton, allowed admission to his gardens free and had 'button-holes always ready', with fresh fruit, cut flowers and excellent teas. However, the turnstile into Castle Gardens – it was removed only in 1981 – was kept busy and the amenities popular until the 1920s, when the gardens declined into a tangled bird sanctuary of overgrown trees and bushes.

A wagonette trip, all male, outside Castle Gardens, late nineteenth century. Note the sign advertising the bowling green and monkey house.

The Castle Gardens Hotel, 1904. The tearooms are beyond the wrought-iron arch on the right.

Castle Villa, built in 1890, once gave entrance to Castle Gardens. It later became a bicycle shop and is now a private house. (Barbara Strachan)

A group at Castle Gardens during the First World War. Mr Cookson is on the left, smoking his pipe.

Castle Gardens, February 2008.

Looking across the Castle Gardens car park towards some of the trees that were planted by Captain Arthur Fitzroy Thompson. All this area was laid out with rose gardens, a menagerie and so on in the nineteenth century.

Knocking down the outbuilding and making a large car park when recent renovations were done disturbed many wood pigeons and owls which had nested there. Miss Alice Jane Livesey recalls an entrance to the 'Castle', as it was called, from what was recently an ironmonger's shop. There was a small zoo with monkeys and coloured birds. In a lean-to greenhouse Mr Clayton, the gardener, grew orchids and a vinery yielded fine grapes, the largest of which were cooked like gooseberries. She recalls a man shouting by the turnstile 'two pence to go in'. Bay trees, hedges, statues, muscovy ducks on a big ornamental pond, well-kept paths, tea, cakes and beer but no rowdiness – all these are part of Miss Livesey's memories. The Castle Gardens retains its popularity, which must always have been thanks to its nodal position.

Empire Day

After celebrations in the morning with a service, bowing or curtseying to the flag, and singing patriotic songs, Empire Day continued after lunch with the village school's walking in crocodile to the seashore at Bispham where they ran races, looked for shells and generally had a good time.

Church Army

Another occasional treat was provided by the Church Army with their 'ham, jam and glory' slogan; an invitation to high tea after coming to the 'penitence form' in services held in the open air if the weather was fine. They also stayed about a week campaigning, accommodated at the farms. After dark, using a magic lantern, they showed slides which were projected on to the big barn door of Old Kilshaw's Farm. The subjects were biblical, Moses in the bulrushes, David and Goliath, but one can imagine it was truly magic to the children and adults who gathered to see the show.

Carleton Gala

Carleton's festivals or galas and those held by other Fylde villages had their origins in trade guilds, which later became livery companies. They were not just a time of rejoicing but an expression of solidarity and support for a particular craft, skill and membership. Many townships still include tableaux and pageantry directly connected with historical incidents in which their ancestors took part. In earlier times these events were eagerly anticipated all year.

'Success to our Gala', 1913. (Norman Cooper)

Prizewinners at Carleton Gala, 1914. The judging was held at Castle Gardens Inn. (Norman Cooper)

A visiting group of Morris dancers at Carleton Gala, c. 1920.

The Lower Green float, 'Butterflies and Flowers', Carleton Gala, 1937.

Carleton Gala, 1938. The Rose Queen is Kathleen Wilkinson, the cushion bearer Gerald Winder.

The programme for Carleton Gala, 1950. (Chris Greave)

★ 0361 ★

CARLETON
GALA & SPORTS

Saturday, 15th. July, 1950

Gala Field, Poulton Road,
Carleton.

PROGRAMME — THREEPENCE

★ ★

(left) The crowning of the Rose Queen, 1949. Jacqueline Carter is seated, with Prince Charming alongside. Britannia is in the background.

(below) Jacqueline Carter, the Rose Queen, in procession, 1949. Chris Gleave is the crown bearer on the right. (Chris Gleave)

The Carleton Flyer, 1949. It was built to look like one of Rowland Emett's wonderfully eccentric railway cartoons. (Chris Gleave)

The Morris dancers at Carleton Gala, 1950. (Pauline Jackson)

Attendants to the Queen Elect, Carleton Gala, 1950. (Pauline Jackson)

Carleton Gala was always held on a Wednesday in June. The scholars collected outside the school and, led by Poulton Brass Band, set off in procession. There was Morris dancing as well as decorated floats and the joyous crowning of the Rose Queen underneath the old iron arch at Castle Gardens. People sat up all night before to make paper roses, to decorate the arch and the lorries, and to groom the horses. The whole village enjoyed the fair afterwards with hobby horses, wing boats and the rare treat of ice cream.

The first gala held after the First World War was 'at Mustows' on fields opposite the Scout hut where now bungalows are built. There were firework displays and races at night – egg and spoon, sack, three-legged, wheelbarrow – with prizes of money. It was a proud day for the Livesey family when one year Kate was crowned queen and presented with a necklace.

Perhaps the two most memorable galas for Carleton people today are those of 1949 and 1950. Spirits were high after a long and dreary Second World War and imagination ran riot.

The old programmes bring it alive. The Gala Field for Carleton Gala and Sports, Saturday 16 July 1949, was on Poulton Road, Carleton (many more fields there then!) and the price of the well-designed brochure was 3*d.* Mrs E. Moorhouse was president and vice-presidents were

A.B. Bithell JP, Councillor J. Carabine and Councillor R.J. Hull. A long list of helpers, more than eighty Carleton residents, followed. Such enthusiasm! And the list, it stated, was not complete 'due to the early writing of the programme'.

'Let us make this second Gala an even greater success than last year's post-war effort.' Looking at the photographs, they did! The *Gazette and Herald* and *Evening Gazette* offered valuable publicity.

On the Gala Day there was a 'pleasant surprise' for all children. Extra Junior Sports were featured, as well as a Comedy Race in the evening. The First Carleton Scouts made their building site available, right across from what must have been Mustow's Field. The Scouts collected parking fees, which went towards their building fund for the handsome hall pictured elsewhere in the book.

The Grand Procession assembled in an orderly manner at Castle Gardens and set off at 10.30am, headed by the police, the Blackpool Liaison Band, Morris dancers, banner bearers and official cars. Once the procession got going marshals and stewards, Messrs Noble, Wilson, Petrie and Rothesey, were kept busy. Examples of tableaux are listed, and fancy dress classes included the most original, the best decorated pram, cycle, the best comic character, the best mounted character and the neatest and best decorated horse. Even the collectors, also in fancy dress, could compete for first, second and third prizes. Britannia, the retiring queen was followed by ladies in waiting, the Rose Queen elect, cushion bearer and crown bearer, Prince Charming and the Carleton Personality Girl. There were also country dancers, maypole dancers and petal throwers.

The route of the procession is interesting and for the walkers on a hot day it would have been demanding: Castle Gardens, Carleton Gate, crematorium, Hawthorne Grove, Rington Avenue and then to the Carleton Memorial Centre.

Miss Elaine Harrison was the retiring queen in 1949 and the Rose Queen was Miss Jacqueline Carter.

Much light is shed by the advertisements in the programme. O. Wood, general draper, had already been established over fifty years, having shops in both Carleton and Poulton.

There were eleven races for the adults in the evening – cycle, flat, potato race, obstacle, hurdle – and it cost 1*s* to enter, although the ladies 100yds open and the 20yds comedy race were free to enter. To round off the day Mr and Mrs Longford, who were then in charge at the Castle Gardens Inn, extended a hearty welcome: 'Come and join us in a singsong'.

An important feature the following year was that winners in all children's events were awarded points, and the child with the most received a gold and silver medal presented by the Carleton Ratepayers Association.

Thornton Gala

Happily Thornton Gala is still with us. Commencing over a century ago as Club Day, it became known as Joy Day. Less of the carnival spirit was displayed in the early days but it became more and more popular as whole families wanted to join in, and by 1927 the procession was reported to be a mile long. About 1,500 children took part wearing fancy dress costumes, some on foot, others on tableaux drawn by well-groomed horses decorated with paper roses and gleaming brasses. There were bands, Morris dancers, decorated bicycles and perambulators and of course the crowning of the Rose Queen. Marquees, swing boats and a greasy pole were erected in the enclosure belonging to Councillor

Poulton Band, seen here in 1872, played at Carleton and other traditional galas in the Fylde.

R. Jenkinson facing the Council Offices, and also in 1927 Bertha Gilliat, a pupil at Beach Road Council School, was crowned Queen.

Yes, those were some of the days in Thornton-Cleveleys, but perhaps the proudest and most carefree was Jubilee Day 1897 when Queen Victoria had ruled over Great Britain and an Empire for sixty years. One of the miller's daughters of Marsh Mill, Thornton, Miss Freeborn, remembered it vividly: 'We dressed in our best and sang a hymn specially composed for the occasion. In the afternoon, in "Queen's weather", we walked down the lanes to the sea.'

Lancaster Fair

One of the rare treats enjoyed every year by Carleton boys and girls was a visit to Lancaster Fair. Reading through the special notices for Fair Day, which was timed to coincide with the August Assizes, gives a good idea of the wealth of incident in store: 'On Fair Day, the Priory and Parish Church of St Mary will be open to visitors from half past nine in the morning until the close of the Fair. . . . The ladies of the Church Refectory beg to inform that they will be serving refreshments from half past ten in the morning until a quarter before nine at night. On Monday, August 27 1808, there will be available, tours of the Castle on the hour and half past the hour from 10.30am until 4pm.'

From Mistress Walmsley's booth in the churchyard nettle beer and refreshing cordials were obtainable and the 'Juggling young gentleman, Thomas Schofield would return to present a new show, more daring than ever before, including dangerous manoeuvres with fire'. Mr Pilling Dick also had renowned booths 'which could provide unrivalled entertainment – a fantastic cabinet of curiosities and an astonishing captured wildman, more ferocious than any other exhibited in captivity'. Of particular note was 'An exceptional mermaid and for the first time at any Fair this year, the True remains of the Head of Oliver Cromwell'. The public were assured by Pilling Dick MA that his entertainment was suitable for 'connoisseurs, scholars and respectable persons of high rank and station'!

Juvenile swinging boats were at the fair under the eagle eye of Mistress Penellum, and the 'triumphant return' of Mr Pentecost Lloyd and his Theatre Company with their 'much-acclaimed performance of the triumph and tragedy of Admiral Lord Nelson', which 'should not be missed': there were five shows a day!

The Corporation of the Borough of Lancaster takes the Liberty of informing its FREEMEN, FRIENDS, SUPPORTERS and the PUBLIC *in general*, that it intends to stage, for one day only on HOLIDAY MONDAY, 27th AUGUST 2001, a *Remarkable and Superior* event, the likes of which will not be seen elsewhere in the Kingdom, *viz*:

The Annual Lancaster
Georgian Festival Fair

Whereby will be celebrated all the *sights, sounds, shows, trials, tribulations* and *characters* of a provincial fair and market set in the year 1808 and to which all TOWNSFOLK and VISITORS are invited without charge.

The whole to take place on the **Castle Green** and in the **Priory Churchyard**, Starting at 11 o'clock prompt in the morning and *to include*:

The return by public demand of Mr. PILLING DICK'S fine Entertainment containing a fantastic and invaluable **Cabinet of Curiosities**, wherein will be exhibited his exceptional Mermaid and for the first time at any fair this year, the *True Remains* of Oliver Cromwell's Head, with other notable rarities & contained adjacent in a secure booth, an Astonishing CAPTURED WILDMAN, more ferocious than any ever seen in captivity and the likes of which will surpass all other spectacles, however amazing.

Never seen before at Lancaster Fair, the Marvellous STROMBOLI will consume and breathe prodigious quantities of fire and swallow swords of great length, assisted by his Lady, SILVIA. They will present, for the first time other than in front of Royalty, the Fantastic and Dangerous WHEEL OF FIRE.

Never seen outside of the Cities of London and Westminster, excepting at Lancaster Fair, the exhibition of the Wonderful Miss Atkinson, the MAGNIFICENT PIG-FACED LADY. A *natural* prodigy of high station and considerable fortune. *This lady should not be confused with divers crude Hog Faced Women and other poor fakes and imitations which have lately been shewn at shows in the northern counties.*

Dr. S. GRIPENERVE *(late physic to the Emperor of all Austria)*, Supplier to Royalty, Nobility & Gentry of Miracle Elixirs and Cures of sterling merit. Exhibitor of Curios and Rare Exotica. All to be presented within his *Magnificent New* TEMPLE OF HEALTH containing many Wonders of Science. The GODDESS EUPHOBIA to portray scenes of exquisite drama and adopt gracious attitudes.

EUNUS the *Fire Eater* will EAT & BREATHE FIRE and repose upon a bed composed entirely of nails.

The Triumphal Return of Mr. PENTECOST LLOYD, and his THEATRE Company, with their much acclaimed performance of – Scenes from the TRIUMPH & TRAGEDY of the DEATH of ADMIRAL LORD NELSON. THE WHOLE presented before painted scenery *which has attracted admiration whenever it has been shewn.*

THOS. SCHOFIELD Esq. the *Juggling Young Gentleman* presents a new show, more daring than before and including the most dangerous manoeuvres wth fire.

The drama of Mr. PUNCH and his wife Joan, presented by PRICE the PUPPETEER

PROFESSOR SHERIDAN, Surgeon and Apothecary, supplier of *Rare Liquid Infusions* & agent for the sale of Messrs. McIver's and Duncan's sheep salve, grease butter, scrapings, etc. etc.

Penellum's SWINGING BOATS to provide *Delight* for the Juvenile Patrons.

For the second time only at this fair, The CONTRETEMPS THEATRE Co. presents its Perennial Popular Entertainment, The TRIALS of HARLEQUIN, with MUSIC selected from the most EMINENT COMPOSERS, with New Comic Scenes, Dresses and other Decorations

Sir Henry Greatham's GRAND THEATRE presents the premier of an epic, and Patriotic Shew, depicting tales in which Britannia's enemies are vanquished! Huzzah!. *All perform'd within a most commodious booth.*

Mr HULBERT & Mr. SHARKEY, will perform, singular *Juggling Tricks, Astonishing Escapes* and *Legerdemain.*

The Renowned Messrs. BROOMHEAD & TAYLOR, Noted Acrobats and *Jugglers.*

The GREAT ARTIZANI to undertake *Death Defying* Feats upon the slackrope.

The Zoroastrian Fortune Teller MYSTIC MIRANDA, most *stunning* in Beauty and Uncanny in her ability to PREDICT THE FUTURE.

And divers other entertainments viz:

Under the patronage of John Dent MP, Madame Leger has been engaged to lead the steps, and will be accompanied by fine music played by the NOISE of MINSTRELS. Also games, side-shows and neat stalls selling the best commodities, produce, victuals and fancy goods, fruit and vegetables; herbs; baskets and besoms; pottery and pewter ware; Candles; pipes and haberdashery. Walmsley's TAVERN OF ABSTINENCE and RADCLIFFE'S SAUSAGE TABLE will be in attendance.

Of particular note and starting at 5 o'clock in the afternoon the
NINTH NATIONAL SEDAN CHAIR CARRYING CHAMPIONSHIPS

The Bellman will proclaim the FAIR at half-past Ten o'clock from Mr. Covell's Cross, a quarter to eleven from the Castle's John O'Gaunt gateway and at 11 o'clock from the Priory Churchyard Sundial, to be followed by the opening of the Fair by the Borough's *Members of Parliament*. Take note also that the REGULAR ARMY will be recruiting for men to serve King and Country and that Miss DUCKETT has again agreed to give lessons for Poor Girls in her Schoolroom, to be established on **Fair Day** in the *Judges' Lodgings.* THE PRIORY CHURCH REFECTORY will be open for refreshment; Tours of the Castle are to be available throughout.

God Save the King

Lancaster Georgian Festival Fair is produced [
Tourist Information Centre and offices at 29 Castle Hill, Lancaster, LA1 1Y
& Old Station Buildings, Marine Road Central, Morecambe, LA4 4DB.

The programme for Lancaster's Georgian Festival Fair in 2001, recreating all the favourite acts from 1808's fair!

Throughout the day news and notices for Fair Day were roared out by the corporation bellman.

The official opening of the fair was by Mr John Dent MP. Friends and supporters were to meet him at the Priory Sundial at 9 o'clock at night to march forth to light the churchyard beacon. Minstrels played and Madame Leger led the dancing. Price the puppeteer gave performances of Punch and Judy. Nearby was James Radcliffe with his sausage table, where the finest meat sausages were grilled over the purest charcoal. Jane Rigby had on sale a large assortment of haberdashery and cheese! Miss Atkinson, the pig-faced lady ('greatest wonder of the age') was not to be confused with 'divers crude, hog-faced women and other fakes'. Shown by Mr Hobbs who was assisted by Mr Dockray, she was normally only seen in London and Westminster. It cost 8s to consult her. What did people ask?

There was a prize lottery at the Ladies Repository. 'Eunus will eat and breathe fire', while Broomhead and Taylor juggled with fire, and Hulbert and Shankey performed tricks of astonishing escapes and legerdemain as the Great Antizani undertook death-defying feats on the slack rope! Nettle beer and frumenty sustained throughout the day, as did gingerbread. This was so popular at fairs and galas throughout the county that it was renamed fairings. Here is a traditional recipe. Ingredients: 10oz flour, 1lb treacle, 12oz butter, 1lb sugar, ¼oz cinnamon, ¼oz mace, ½oz ground ginger, a little grated lemon rind. Melt butter and mix with treacle and sugar. Add flour, lemon, mace, cinnamon and ginger. Beat mixture well. Drop very thinly on a well-greased tin and bake in a moderate oven. Cut into squares. Curl each round your finger. Keep in a tin.

It is interesting to note that at this time, 1808, fear of Napoleon Bonaparte was greatly in evidence even at the Fair. There was a notice 'to all aspiring heroes bold' – all lovers of 'Liberty and roast beef' were urged to make for the parade yard at the Castle on Fair Day, where 'each with a desire to bear arms would be kindly entertained . . . besides which you shall receive ten shillings advance and a crown to drink his Majesty's health, new hats, caps, arms, cloth and accoutrements. Apply to Captain Middleton of the 48th Foot.' One wonders if any Carleton boys in search of adventure were tempted on that day 200 years ago to change from plough boy to soldier boy.

Typically well-loaded wagonettes visit the Bull Hotel, Poulton, on an excursion in the late nineteenth century. Crowds of children used to await the mail coaches here in earlier times.

Wakes Weeks

With the steady passage of time, during which conditions have changed radically, whole textile communities have died out. Wakes traditions have also altered. Chorley, Leyland and Preston, once dead towns from the third Saturday in July, in 1952 introduced two holiday weeks overlapping with other textile towns. Overloaded Wakes Weeks had caused problems over travel and holiday accommodation, although a new generation was growing up, taking for granted holidays with pay. For our grandparents the Wakes began on a Saturday, a working day. Holiday Club money was all they had to spend, no wages being paid for the week off. On return it was a case of tighten the belt till pay day, something dreaded by mothers with children to feed.

Even the colliery horses were remembered, being brought to the surface of the mine to enjoy a week's daylight for the only time in the year.

Blackpool, Morecambe, Southport and the Isle of Man have had to give way to the Costa del Sol, Cyprus and the Canaries, but old customs die hard. Doggedly, some towns retain their annual, time-honoured exodus even if they are not so widespread as before. With hijacking, terrorism and war, places like Blackpool are coming back into their own.

Before the full week off was instituted, Manchester men went to the Races, Manchester women to the Markets and the Royal Exchange, gazing into shop windows, so that Whit Saturday became known as 'Gaping Saturday'.

The first man to get drunk at the Wake was dubbed mayor for the day. The Rev. Mr Hull in Poulton-le-Fylde, a market town with fifteen inns, put a stop to this. Imagine what it was like in Preston in 1834 with a population of 50,000 and 190 inns. No wonder the temperance movement started in Preston, at the Old Cockpit built by the Earl of Derby. Here the population had enjoyed the 'sport' of cock fighting as part of the Wake.

Among the 'sports', many of them designed to raise a laugh, were eating hasty pudding; smoking tobacco; drinking very hot tea (at which the old ladies were best). There was a prize 'for the first person to finish a plate of hot porridge and treacle eaten sitting on the church step'.

And then there was the rush-bearing ceremony, which originated long ago when the church floor was strewn with rushes to keep out the cold. Cut from the river banks, the rushes were ceremonially borne through the streets of the villages, a good excuse for drinking home-brewed beer afterwards. In time the ceremony devolved to the children. It was always held on the Sunday nearest to 5 August, St Oswald's Day. Rochdale traditionally still mounts an elaborate rush cart for its procession. The Long Morris, danced by men in wooden clogs, usually led the rushcart processions held during Wakes Weeks.

Trinity Wake Week fare included ham, plum pudding, stuffed bacon chine, wake-pudding and ginger beer. Wake pudding was made of bread and butter, eggs, milk, sugar, suet, currants and peel. In Cheshire frumenty was the main Wake dish and at Westhoughton special pork pasties were baked and people came from miles on the baking day. Olives were considered part of festival fare. They were thin slices of veal stuffed with sage; mention of them was made as far back as the seventeenth century. Beef olives are presumably in direct descent.

Lancashire Wakes Cakes were also a traditional food – and here is a traditional recipe for them. Ingredients: 8oz plain flour, 4oz butter, 5oz sugar, 1 large free-range egg, 1oz currants, milk to mix. Rub fat into flour. Stir in sugar and currants. Mix to a stiff dough with beaten egg and milk. Knead until smooth and roll out dough to 1 in thick, cutting into rounds. Place on a greased baking sheet and cook in a moderate oven for fifteen minutes or until golden brown. Cool on wire tray, dredging generously with sparkling sugar.

Over-eating at the Wakes and other festivals sent people to consult old herbals. In the seventeenth century Gerard suggested that one should 'put caraway seeds amongst baked fruits and cakes to help digest wind'.

Chapter Eleven
STORMY WEATHER

The Huntcliff

Of all the ships that have foundered on the coast of Lancashire in memorable storms one of the luckiest 'landings' was that of the *Huntcliff* in February 1894. Such was the wind and the flood of seas inland that rabbits and hares were seen running down the streets of Lytham, driven from their sandhills home. Large advertising boards were uprooted and carried away, and lead was ripped from roofs, but all such incidents paled into insignificance when compared with the stranding of the steamship *Huntcliff* on the 12th.

She was a cargo boat for which George Horsley and Sons of Hartlepool had paid £36,000 only two years before – an ocean tramp' 350ft in length and with a registered tonnage of 2,018. The crew consisted of twenty-seven men, the Wilkes brothers of Middlesbrough being in charge of the magnificent 1,700hp engines. Five Arabs and a Zulu looked after the stoking – and there were two stowaways on board.

Having made the run from Java to New York with sugar, *Huntcliff* had come to Liverpool with a cargo of cotton. Bound for Cardiff, where she planned to load coals at Barry Dock for Aden, she left Liverpool at 2 o'clock on Sunday only carrying water ballast, and with a pilot on board. Absence of a cargo meant that a tremendous amount of hull was exposed to the violence of wind and waves; and at 5 o'clock, when she

The Huntcliff *at St Annes, before her refloating, 1894.*

was just about 4 miles off Great Orme, gales began.

Despite her weight and size, the vessel was swung around with ease, for the rudder had no hold on the water, and when sails were set to keep her 'head on' the canvas was torn from the rigging like paper. Captain Howell and Chief Officer Peterson decided to lie as near to the coast of Llandudno as they could, and so dropped anchor. Their plan failed. Worse still, the anchor could not be hauled up again, and 120 fathoms of chain had to be sacrificed to the angry sea. They could neither shelter nor put back to Liverpool. Broadside on, the *Huntcliff* rolled so fearfully that the crew had a hard time holding on. Terrified, the stowaways – who had thought only of a free passage to Cardiff – dearly wished they had never come.

Between 5 o'clock on Sunday afternoon and 2 o'clock on Monday morning the *Huntcliff* was blown at the caprice of the elements, until she bumped at St Annes. Finally the vessel was deposited, quite undamaged, on the sandy beach not far from the Convalescent Home and only 50yds from the sandhills. Not one of her steel plates was buckled. A better place for beaching could not have been chosen, and there was many a joke afterwards to the effect that *Huntcliff* was her name and she lived up to it.

News of the stranding of such a magnificent boat travelled fast. Crowds poured in from all over the district, and professional

The first St Annes lifeboat, **Laura Janet,** *and her crew, nineteenth century. (Patrick Ramsey)*

The new St Annes lifeboat, 2007. (Patrick Ramsey)

***Collecting for Lifeboat Saturday, 1926 – an important event all along the
Lancashire coast.***

photographers swarmed alongside amateurs. At high tide clouds of spray
broke over the decks, and spectators venturing near received a soaking.
Ice cream stalls and fruit sellers set up (in February!), and by Wednesday
the immediate area around the vessel was described as a veritable
fairground. Many visitors were brought in by railway, but so great was the
crowd that few were allowed on board. No doubt there were souvenir
hunters galore; and someone set up a collecting box for the Convalescent
Home opposite the stranded steamer.

Meanwhile discussions about moving *Huntcliff* continued. As the
vessel was insured for £35,000 the underwriters were determined to
refloat her! Should a channel be dug for her passage to the sea? Or
perhaps a slip could be constructed, and she could be lifted with
hydraulic jacks – allowing her to be refloated on the 28ft tide expected on
20 February.

On the 24th they eventually managed it. Meanwhile the Arabs had
been embroiled in a knife fight ashore, while another crew member had
been found incapable on the genteel pavement of St Annes 'with a bottle
of whiskey for a pillow'. So it was that ship's crew and townspeople alike
breathed a sigh of relief as *Huntcliff* finally sailed off towards Liverpool.

Clara

Another crowd-puller was the barque *Clara*, wrecked in December 1906 on her way from Norway to Preseton, a trip she had made without mishap on twenty-four previous occasions. The captain of this 430 ton wooden barque tried to obtain a pilot a mile south of Nelson Buoy, but without success. At midnight in a heavy squall her keel struck bottom. Continual bumping caused the rudder to break and the mainsail crashed down, carrying away the sails. Seeing that capsize was imminent, the crew took to the ship's boat, but were blown helplessly over the treacherous sandbanks until landed by the Fleetwood lifeboat at 8am. The lifeboat signal gun brought hundreds on to the Promenade to watch the drama unfold, and although it was winter subsequent weeks saw extra trains running on the Preston and Wyre Railway, bringing in the sightseers.

Riverdance

'The beached vessel has attracted a steady stream of onlookers.' As I wrote this chapter I heard television news reporting that the *Riverdance*, a ferry making regular sailings between Ireland and Heysham, has gone aground off Norbreck, Blackpool (31 January 2008). In severe weather conditions a freak wave caused the ferry to move so erratically that containers toppled, some breaking open, causing *Riverdance* to list heavily. Gales of 70mph made rescue operations almost impossible. Weather was described as 'horrendous', but the passengers and eventually the crew, who had stayed on board hoping to secure the cargo, had all to be winched off. That was a dangerous but fortunately successful time. The helicopters, some from as far away as Anglesey, effected a magnificent rescue operation. The fear was of pollution from oil-spill, but the *Riverdance* cargo, comprising scrap metal, timber and potting compost, was itself non-polluting.

History along the Fylde coast repeats itself. As always, drama at sea in storm and tempest with its subsequent casualties 'pulls the crowds'. As with the grounding of that magnificent steamship *Huntcliff* in 1894 it appeared that righting *Riverdance* would take some time to solve.

What can compare with the primal power of the elements against one ship, to stir the blood and play upon the full range of human emotions? It may be surprising, but man set sail long before he sat on a horse or trudged behind a wheel.

Two views of Riverdance, *February 2008 – when the wreck was described as 'one of the Fylde's biggest tourist attractions'. (Ted Ramsey)*

Chapter Twelve
SCOUTS AND GUIDES

The 1ˢᵗ Carleton Boy Scout Group was first registered at Scout Headquarters, Stella Maris, Westfield Avenue, Little Carleton, on 10 January 1927. The Scoutmaster was Mrs Harriet A. Brown and there were six scouts. This was originally in Blackpool District but passed to Wyre District on 5 April 1967. The Boy Scouts Association's *Weekly News Bulletin* on 8 December 1942 issued an article which made every scout in Great and Little Carleton swell with pride for one of its number:

Cornwell Badge for invalid scout who kicked the 'Im' out of 'Impossible'. Tony Hewitson is an invalid. He could not join other boys in their games, could not even go to school. Only when the weather was really favourable could he leave his room for an excursion out of doors. The Scoutmaster of the local Boy Scout Troop took the invalid some copies of *The Scout*, and discovered that the boy was longing to be a Scout. To the Scoutmaster's surprise, Tony knew the tests for the Tenderfoot Badge – he had learnt them from the Scout handbook, *Scouting for Boys*. The following week with some Scouts round his bedside, Tony made the Scout Promise. He became a Handicapped Scout, attached to the 1ˢᵗ Carleton Troop, Blackpool. Unable to attend Troop meetings because any

An empty Poulton Road, late 1890s. The Scout Hut is now on the left.
(Norman Cooper)

Carleton Cubs and Scouts. The lady cubmaster is Vera Potter.
(Pauline Jackson)

undue excitement would be dangerous, Tony carried on his Scouting at home, visited by his Scoutmaster and members of the troop. He passed test after test until he had obtained his First Class Badge. His devoted mother was his patient for his practice in First Aid. Unable to use his signalling flags, Tony transmitted a message in pin-man drawings, and in that way passed his semaphore signalling test. Every obstacle towards Scouting efficiency Tony overcame, and he has been an example to the normal boys of his Troop. Tony hasn't the strength to whistle, but he knows how to smile. For nine long years he has borne his increasing suffering courageously and with fortitude. Tony has been awarded the Cornwell badge of the Boy Scouts Association in recognition of his high courage, determination and character: 'Cornwell Scout Badge Anthony Hewitson 1st Class Scout 1942 1st Carleton (Blackpool). In recognition of his high standard of character and devotion to duty over nine years, under great suffering. Although only sixteen Hewitson has been ill for nine years and has undergone much weariness and suffering during that long period but he has always remained cheerful and has born his trials with great fortitude and a smile. In spite of his many difficulties he has succeeded through sheer dogged perseverance in becoming a 1st Class Scout.

Carleton 1st and 2nd Brownies with the 1st and 2nd Guides, 1985.
(Pauline Jackson)

Chapter Thirteen
CHURCHES TOGETHER
(by Graham Baines, churchwarden)

St Martin de Porres

This brief history of St Martin de Porres Church covers the period from its inception in 1964 until 1998, when it became St Martin de Porres and St Hilda of Whitby under the shared church arrangements entered into with the Church of England community in Carleton.

In the early 1960s there was no Catholic church in Carleton, and since few people had cars it was often difficult for Catholic residents to get to mass at St John the Evangelist in Poulton. Thus in February 1963 a Mass Centre was started in the Scout Hut, Poulton Road, Carleton, with the first mass being celebrated by Father John Bamber, the parish priest of St John's. The Sunday mass was generally attended by some forty to fifty parishioners.

The use of the Scout Hut was much appreciated, but with Carleton's increasing population and the consequent increase in the number of Catholic residents, it was recognised that a purpose-built church was required.

Following a census of Carleton's Catholic population a committee was formed to build up the spiritual and social life of the Carleton area, with the first meeting being held on 26 August 1963. Various fundraising

The Scout Hut, Carleton

events were arranged to raise funds for the building of a chapel– whist drives, jumble sales, raffles, hot pot suppers and garden parties. Land on Fleetwood Road, adjoining the Castle Gardens Hotel, was earmarked, and permission to build was granted by the local authority in November 1963.

Carleton's chapel of ease, dedicated to St Martin de Porres (a saint who cared for the sick and needy), was completed on 3 July 1964 at a cost of about £6,500, and opened by Bishop Foley, of the Lancaster diocese, on Sunday 2 August 1964. The dedication was chosen by a ballot of parishioners: it is not known why St Martin de Porres was so popular!

The chapel has continued to be served by the clergy of St John's, Poulton; the first of these was Father Bamber. While the spiritual life of St Martin's has remained under the wing of St John's, its social life has always been organised by St Martin's parishioners. One highlight was the flower festival arranged in 1989 by Kathleen Swarbrick, to mark the chapel's twenty-fifth anniversary.

St Hilda of Whitby

On 22 September 1680 Elizabeth Wilson of Whiteholme made her will. In it a quarter of her goods were bestowed in land, the rent of which was to be used for the education of poor children in Carleton.

Further bequests followed, and by 1697 a schoolhouse had been built at Four Lane Ends. In 1839 another school was built on the site,

A service in St Chad's Church for pupils of Carleton School, 1983. (Miss J.M. Partington)

and this was followed by a larger red brick building in 1902. Here, sixty-three years later, Carleton Church was born: the records of St Chad's PCC record that on Sunday 19 September 1965 a family communion service began in Carleton School Hall.

In 1927 William Pye had given some land at Pye's Farm to the Church, with the 'long term objective of building a permanent church'. There was little action in this respect until April 1970, when the vicar referred to the possibility of using this plot as building land: the diocese had agreed in principle for Carleton to have a priest in charge and for the old school (vacant since 1967, when a new school had been built further down Bispham Road) to be converted into a church. However, in 1972 it was decided that it would be 'impossible for the people to build and maintain a church', and in 1974 the land was sold off. Finally, in 1981, further discussion with the Bishop of Lancaster resulted in Carleton receiving its first curate in charge; a house in Roylen Avenue, now known as Church House, was provided for him and his wife. Weekly services were established in the 'new' school in September 1983, and in May 1984 the Carleton Church Choir was formed to sing at the weekly Sunday service. The choir continues to this day to lead and enhance worship.

In the early 1990s a number of options were being explored regarding the future of Carleton Church – building a new church on land in Arundel Drive or on land within the school grounds, for example. In 1993 the first generous offer was made to share the Roman Catholic church of St Martin de Porres. Discussions continued, and on 6 September 1995 Carleton Church held its first mid-week service at St Martin's Church – although services also continued at the school.

Social links between the two churches continued to grow, and ecumenical services took place. Friendship and trust were developing all the time. At this point another formal approach was made to discuss sharing St Martin's. 'Just bring yourselves' was the generous offer. In June 1998 Carleton Church unanimously agreed to change its name to St Hilda of Whitby, and the church school followed suit soon afterwards.

St Martin and St Hilda

On Friday 11 September 1998 a service of unity and commitment was held at the church of St Martin and St Hilda. Since then the church has been run jointly, with shared ecumenical services, retreats, Bible studies and a wide range of social activities all cementing friendships between the two communities. For the last ten years Anglicans and Catholics have worked together in Carleton as a single community, holding much in common and making a real difference to the people of Carleton.

St Martin and St Hilda's Church and church hall, Great Carleton, 2008.

Chapter Fourteen
SHOPS AND BUSINESSES

Yesterday

Whereas long before 1900 farming dominated the acres of Great and Little Carleton, half a century later shopkeepers were getting busy. Advertisements from 1950 reveal a surprising number of shops and flourishing businesses. E.C. Langford at the Castle Gardens Hotel and café called himself the 'Thirst Aid Specialist', with 'scores of remedies for relaxed throats, jaded appetites, tired nerves and that sinking feeling'. His advice was given freely to all visiting 'The homely house where all are welcome'. The Castle was a popular meeting place. At 8 Blackpool Road, Carleton, Gordon Wilson, a ladies' and gentleman's hairdresser, offered Jamal and Createx permanent waving. There was a general stores at 21 Poulton Road, Great Carleton, presided over by Mr Roughley. Food rationing was still in force, and he states, 'We supply all rationed goods'. He himself manufactured Fyldezone bleach, as well as selling greeting cards, Platignum pens and wallpaper to 'discerning housewives'. Colin S. Craven was a plumber, glazier and sanitary engineer. At 267 Blackpool Old Road near Carleton railway crossing, Haldon Thompson's Trading Company was the place to buy linoleum. E. Richards and Son of Market Place, Poulton-le-Fylde, was the oldest ironmonger in the Fylde, established in 1754, and all the farmers went there for supplies.

Carleton Garage, 1920. The 'Garage for 50 Cars' was at Four Lane Ends, opposite Castle Gardens.

W.H. Brook, Carleton newsagent and stationer in the 1920s.

(left) Brook's later became Harry Gleave Ltd. This photograph probably dates from 1964, a year after Mr Gleave took over the business. (Chris Gleave)

(below) Henderson's Dining Room and fish and chip shop is next door.

'Everything in the hardware line' was stocked at Richards' 'ironmongers, tool dealers and farmers' stores. Locksmiths and lawn mower repair service'. Sad to say, they are no longer available. Ashwell's were at Great Carleton Post Office, and were also grocers and provision dealers, selling sweets, tobacco, minerals and ice-cream. At 15 Rington Avenue was John Thompson the chemist, also a qualified ophthalmic optician. All kinds of building work was undertaken and plant could be hired at N.A. Robson Ltd, builders, contractors and quarrymasters: 60 Fleetwood Road, Carleton, was their premises. Marshall's Motors (Carleton Ltd) was opposite Castle Gardens. The motor car was coming out of the garage after petrol rationing for 'repairs, service and lubrication'.

Clinnings high-class mineral waters were on sale throughout the district, and on Gala Day were sold all day long on the Gala Field. Their great rival was C&S XL Ales (the C and S standing for Catterall and Swarbrick), which supplied the Castle Gardens Hotel. Beevers made wreaths, bouquets and floral tributes at their premises at 115 Bispham Road, Carleton. Clixo's shop opposite the school was popular with the children on Gala Day. 'Open all day' was Henderson's – 'right in the heart of Carleton for fish that is fresh daily – our fish and chips are delicious'. It is interesting to note also that the nearest department store to Carleton was RHO Hills, Blackpool, which was open most nights until 10pm.

Today

In the twenty-first century many family-run businesses and shops have had to close, unable to compete with the supermarket giants, but Carleton has been most fortunate (apart from the loss of its post office, a fate shared by hundreds of sub-post offices throughout the land). Indeed in the year before writing Carleton has seen shops opened and doing well. We now have a delicatessen, Salt of the Earth, another hairdressing salon and a physiotherapist to add to butcher, baker, newsagent, florist and fruiterer, pharmacy, doctors' surgery, furniture and upholstery, garage, off-licence, mini-market and the refurbished Castle Gardens, which soldiers on splendidly providing snacks, lunches and evening meals. Away from the larger towns, few smaller communities can boast such amenities. We hope this may long continue, fostered as it is by a community spirit desirous of patronising local shops and businesses because we value the friendship, the good feeling built into this state of

Salt of the Earth opened in 2007.

Carleton News and Carleton Pharmacy, February 2008.

The small and handy supermarket in Great Carleton.

affairs. Local associations – bowling, gardening, thriving churches, Girl Guides, keep fit, local history society, rate payers' association and so on heartily encourage community cohesion: in many areas shop after shop has been sacrificed and the heart of the community has died. Such a state of affairs is particularly devastating to the elderly. I say that SOS means Save Our Shops, and we in Great and Little Carleton mean to do just that.

Chapter Fifteen
FROM DUG-OUT TO DES RES

Changing Times

Lytham residents have recently viewed with some dismay the prospect of sweeping changes to their much loved and cherished town. The cry goes up that 'More houses are needed', and those who question this are told that 'You cannot stop progress' – the hackneyed phrase that excuses almost anything. But nothing can still the longings arising from a familiar and annealing past if buildings are razed, if scenery is swept aside and lost forever, changing almost overnight. Blotting out history triggers alarm.

On a gusty, clear day of blue skies and billowing big white clouds I walked along Lytham's promenade, passing the white windmill, Lytham's trademark on the splendid Green. Beyond lay the seemingly infinite horizon as the road sweeps left towards Preston. Suddenly the changed appearance of things familiar was startling. Cookson's Bakery and other landmarks had disappeared, gone – exchanged for T.S. Eliot's Wasteland. Sudden shock and the pangs that go with it hit both consciousness and memory. This area once held some of Lytham's fame and a reputation that travelled thousands of miles, to Chile, Egypt, India, Brazil, Africa and elsewhere. Between 1894 and 1912 the Lytham Shipbuilding and Engineering Company, England, built thirty-five river steamers for South America alone. From time immemorial man has built

Lytham Docks. (Lytham Heritage)

The diesel motor tug Northop, *built by the Lytham Shipbuilding and Engineering Company. (Lytham Heritage)*

'Entrance to the River Wyre at low water', a lithograph by William Gawin Herdman, 1829.

ships. One sea captain called the River Ribble 'infernal', but since primitive man hewed and shaped by fire the first dug-out canoes and coracles, craft and vessels for sailing on water have continued to be made. One has to except the Romans, for although they used the River Ribble and were thought to land at Freckleton Naze they were not associated with the building of ships in Britain. Messrs Allansons had a shipyard on the salt pool of the Ribble not far away from an old ford at Freckleton where stood the ancient Bush Inn. This was a useful yard, but Lytham's 'going down to the sea in ships' was worldwide. Long useful as a calling place for small passenger steamers and pleasure boats, Lytham's chances were fancied in 1830 by the Lord of the Manor, Thomas Clifton, as the much-needed port of refuge on the Fylde coast but that was not to be. Peter Hesketh's generous and extravagant proposals - railways, docks, quays, new town and Captain Henry Mangles Denham's charting of the River Wyre ('classed safe and easy') won the day, and Fleetwood was chosen instead, and the Preston and Wyre railway was built to Preston. However, the Ribble Navigation Company of those days did come to an agreement with Mr Clifton for the making of a dock and wharves. The site at Lytham Creek near the end of the promenade set the shipyard on the Lytham side of Liggard Brook. By 1893 Richard Smith and Company had become Lytham Shipbuilding and Engineering Ltd, England. The site covered 9 acres and well I remember the charming motive power museum with its length of narrow gauge railway track and refurbished coaches which appeared in the declining years. Whatever happened to it?

Family outings were so enjoyable for my husband was alive then, and from the greatest to the least we were all keen train spotters. Trips to Dock Road were fun. All that was after the glory days of shipbuilding when sturdy steamers were launched, some travelling as far as the River Amazon for their sterling work. Their names read like a resounding roll call from a poem by John Masefield – *Mungo Park, Mystic, Pioneer, Sunlight Wasp, Prince George, Cumbria, Fylde, Cecil, Resolute, Vulcan, John Millar.* There were ketches, schooners, iron barques and single screw steamers. *Toiler* and *Amazon* served their country in the First World War and in the Second World War Mulberry Harbour sections built for the Admiralty were towed off from Lytham. One of the first ships built was *Zaire*, later used in the film *Sanders of the River*, featuring Paul Robeson. One of the last was *Drake*, the chain ferry used on Windermere in the Lake District. In July 1955 plant, machinery and equipment at the premises in Dock Road were auctioned off, ending employment for 400 men and a vital industry that had done well for Lytham over many years. The site is at present used for a weekly open market held on Saturdays. Fylde Borough Council, amid some fierce opposition, is considering Kensington Developments' planning application for a housing development complex in the Dock Road/Preston Road area of Lytham, with 40 per cent affordable dwellings.

The Carleton Community Association

As Carleton changes in so many ways, it becomes more and more important that its life as a vibrant community is sustained – and the role of the Carleton Community Association becomes yet more crucial. Its precursor was formed on 17 September 1945, commencing with a shoe-string budget of £5. Trustees were appointed who managed to buy land from a local resident after struggling to raise the necessary £200. Weeton Army Camp supplied a wooden building which was

A celebration procession to mark VJ Day, 1945. (Norman Cooper)

brought to the new area of land. What pride, for it meant that Carleton had its first village hall. A small brick extension which became a kitchen was added in the 1960s. How useful that little hall was to prove! All manner of meetings, shows, parties, educational classes and refuge for senior citizens – all these it made possible. In the early 1980s Carleton Youth and Community Association (CYCA) was formed, the aim being to provide facilities for Carleton's young men and women.

Over the next seventeen years CYCA arranged many events to raise funds for a new hall. It was on 31 March 1994 that the two associations merged to form the Carleton Community Association. Plans for a new building were drawn up but several thousand pounds were necessary for the ambitious project to go forward. Fortunately a lottery grant of £25,000 was forthcoming along with £3,000 from Skelton Bounty. Finally £1,500 was given by ACRE (Action with Communities in Rural England), and the new brick building opened in September 1996. All sections of the community (Over 60's Club, Women's Institute, Slimming World and the Fuschia Society) have benefited. Karate, yoga, pilates and tai chi classes have all found it a useful venue and children's parties have been very popular at weekends.

CCA is making a great contribution to the local community, one that is growing annually, and it is a good example of how, with goodwill, effort and determination, burgeoning success can spring from such small beginnings. The hall was declared ten years old on Saturday 2 September 2006, the pride of Moorfield Avenue.

Chapter Sixteen
PAST, PRESENT AND FUTURE

*F*ollowing hundreds of years of comparatively little change, apart from sporadic modern house building and the demolition of cottage property, which after three centuries was ready to be condemned, Carleton saw its greatest plan in a residential development known as Carleton Green. On 16 May 1973 at the Imperial Hotel, Blackpool, by direction of the Secretary of State for the Environment, 60.97 acres, most of then annexed to Kilshaws and Lower Kilshaws Farms, were offered at auction

Carleton, 1900. The girls have passed Parkinson's corner shop and are level with Old Kilshaw's Farm.

Old Poulton View Farm dates from the seventeenth or eighteenth century. It was used for storing hay when the new Poulton View Farm was built, at right angles.

The new Poulton View Farm, a typical yeoman farmer's dwelling, was built in 1892.

This ancient cobbled wall was a boundary of the old Poulton View Farm. The photograph was taken in 2008.

Lytham Hall, home of the Clifton family, one of the grander Fylde buildings. (Ron Loomes)

A thatched and cruck-built cottage in Clifton Road, 1955.

Carleton Memorial Hall. (Barbara Strachan)

Carleton Bowling Club, 1918.

A harvest supper at the shared church of St Hilda and St Martin – an indication of Carleton's strong community spirit.

by J. Entwistle & Co. Just what change this spread of 562 houses effected – the seven planned shops were not built – can be seen by glancing at the 1892 Ordnance Survey map. This shows acres of differently shaped fields, pocked by marl pits which are now filled in. Every farm used to have its own marl pit, a deep-dug hollow where clay was hoarded ready for spreading as fertiliser. 'Clay on sand makes land' was once a time-honoured Fylde farmers' belief.

Names leap from the uncluttered broad acres of the late nineteenth-century map: Poulton View Farm, Cottam Hall, Woodhead Farm, Carleton Lodge, Old Ryscar, New Ryscar. Apart from the small well-wooded cluster round Great Carleton and the long straight track of railway cutting through the countryside, there is little else recorded, but the firms of Norwest Housing, Wimpey and Moore changed all that between 1973 and 1980. It is therefore not surprising that plans for another housing estate met with fierce opposition. A public meeting called by the Carleton Action group pledged to protect the remaining green belt round the village, and was informed in December 1982 that the Ministry of Agriculture had also objected, which might lead to the scrapping of plans. Gathered in Carleton Memorial Hall, 150 residents were unanimous in their opposition, many feeling that too much high-density housing had been built already. Behind this reasoning was the genuine fear that a close-knit community with identity and character can be lost in spreading suburbia. Faceless anonymity and loneliness proliferate in a concentration of bricks and mortar, as against the community spirit in areas with a nucleus where people know each other. Fears for the Carleton Green land were expressed in the *West Lancashire Evening Gazette* of 22 December 1972, and a study highlighted the isolation of pensioners who had retired to the Fylde.

In protecting and encouraging local history are we indeed hanging on doggedly to our own identities? It matters that we know that Horseman's Hill was once part of Carleton, that it was transferred to Bispham in 1875, that it had long been farmed by Bispham Grange which itself happens to have been one of the oldest farm sites of any in the Fylde, probably going back to monastic times. It is good to know that Thomas Smith, tenant of Norbreck House around 1800, was born in Carleton, that Edwin Waugh, famous Lancashire dialect writer, knew Thomas as 'Owd England', weather-beaten shrimper and farming character that he was; also that the present Anchorsholme Lane was once called

Cockerham Lane, leading over lonely Thornton Marsh, and that the Ladies' Bowling Club occupied Leach Meadow, not far from where the cuckstool was situated! In 1984 the Federation of Family History Societies had only twelve members; now there are well over a hundred. There is a comforting continuity about life when we identify with friends and neighbours of generations ago. Protecting our heritage and seeking out roots is an absorbing pastime, and perhaps its most rewarding facet is that in searching the past we find friends of like minds in the present and the future.

Lucky the donkey was one of old Carleton's characters, who used to enjoy pulling clothes from washing lines, and sometimes eating them, at Little Poulton Farm where Lucky mingled with the seaside donkeys who wintered there. Lucky often escaped his field and could be found wandering as far away as Thornton. (Nicola Waring)

Printed in the United Kingdom
by Lightning Source UK Ltd.
132646UK00001B/55-186/P

9 781